God's Spoken Word
In Plain View

God's Spoken Word In Plain View

Jimmy Jordan - The Messenger

authorHOUSE®

AuthorHouse™ LLC
1663 Liberty Drive
Bloomington, IN 47403
www.authorhouse.com
Phone: 1-800-839-8640

© 2013 by Jimmy Jordan - The Messenger. All rights reserved.

No part of this book may be reproduced, stored in a retrieval system, or transmitted by any means without the written permission of the author.

Published by AuthorHouse   12/19/2013

ISBN: 978-1-4918-1614-1 (sc)
ISBN: 978-1-4918-1593-9 (hc)
ISBN: 978-1-4918-1613-4 (e)

Library of Congress Control Number: 2013916380

Any people depicted in stock imagery provided by Thinkstock are models, and such images are being used for illustrative purposes only.
Certain stock imagery © Thinkstock.

This book is printed on acid-free paper.

Because of the dynamic nature of the Internet, any web addresses or links contained in this book may have changed since publication and may no longer be valid. The views expressed in this work are solely those of the author and do not necessarily reflect the views of the publisher, and the publisher hereby disclaims any responsibility for them.

Dedication

This book is dedicated to my parents, Ethel & James Jordan, firm believers in God's word, who lived their lives as true Christians.

They would help anyone who was in need and would give their last if they were asked to.

They are what you would call "True Blue", real followers of God with a spirit of love and authentic faith in God. I thank God for them and I thank them for instilling the word of God in me and teaching our entire family about Jesus and how to live right.

I learned how to live right just by watching them live their lives. They have taught me by being living examples.

I was taught to always put God first in my life. I was also taught to give and help others. I thank my father for staying by my mother's side through the good and the bad times. He was there, and it's through them that I was taught how to be a good man, live a peaceful life, work for a living and do what's right.

These are the things I was taught and it's because of them and their inspiration . . . I live right and think Godly thoughts. To both of you, I say thank you.

This book is also dedicated to a faithful and longtime friend, Donna Coney, who is near and dear to my heart. Donna has been by my side during the good and the bad times.

She has been there to show me how much she cares for me. She also taught me how to be a more loving person and how to share and be more concerned about others.

I thank her for the times she was faithful to me; sharing her love, thoughts, and tears down through the years.
I thank her for helping me see my flaws and character defects, so that I may be able to change my wrongs into rights. So, through the words in this book, I offer my gift to you.

I hope that this book will inspire you to always give life your best. May God bless you, and may you all bless God!

Table of Contents

Chapter 1: Striving To Stay Focused 1
Chapter 2: God Spoken Word in Plain View 9
Chapter 3: Professing to be a Christian and Reluctant to be Obedient 16
Chapter 4: Walking On the Edge of Life 25
Chapter 5: Giving Life And Dying at the Same Time 32
Chapter 6: A New Life 41
Chapter 7: Never Knew a Love That Could Do So Many Things 49
Chapter 8: Don't Stop, Keep Running For Jesus Until You Drop 58
Chapter 9: Keep the Lights On Listen For My Knock 66
Chapter 10: Yesterday Is Gone 77
Chapter 11: I Know a Man Who Specializes In Junk 87
Chapter 12: Redeem With the Precious Blood of Jesus Christ 96
Chapter 13: Rise Above the Flood 105
Chapter 14: The Burden Bearer 113
Chapter 15: Salvation is free 118
Chapter 16: Victimized by Devices 127

Chapter 17:	He Changed Me	134
Chapter 18:	Displaying More Determination and Less Frustration	137
Chapter 19:	Open Your Eye's And Wake Up	145
Chapter 20:	God Opened My Eyes and Let Me See I Was Naked	149
Chapter 21:	The Good and the Bad	156
Chapter 22:	Good Hearted People with Bad Minds	163
Chapter 23:	Let go of the bad things in your Past	170
Chapter 24:	Grab A Hold Of The Good Things In Your Present Life	170
Chapter 25:	Trust and Obey	179
Chapter 26:	Believing and Succeeding	187
Chapter 27:	Walking Worthy	193
Chapter 28:	God Way Is The Best Way	199
Chapter 29:	Dying To The Sinful Things Of This World	205
Chapter 30:	Take Nothing For Granted	209
Chapter 31:	If we love God like we say we do why we do the things He hates	215
Chapter 32:	Stand	223
Chapter 33:	Perishing from the lack of knowledge	230
Chapter 34:	Pay day is coming	237
Chapter 35:	Turn or Burn	244
Chapter 36:	Stolen Jewels Seize And Kept For Evidence	252

Chapter 37:	He already knows and has already fixed it	261
Chapter 38:	There is strength in repentance	269
Chapter 39:	Looking through the eyes of Jesus	275
Chapter 40:	A Tribute to Dr. Martin Luther King Jr. It's a new day America	281
Chapter 41:	Feet Shod With The Preparation Of The Gospel Peace	287
Chapter 42:	Forever Being Taught and Never Learning	291
Chapter 43:	GOD is a Jealous God	297
Chapter 44:	It's a shortages in the power system	303
Chapter 45:	Being about God's Business	306

Introduction

May you take heed to the words you read! Trust and believe these teachings. Focus in on what is really being said.

Grab hold of the knowledge that is being presented to you. If you snooze, you will lose. Open your eyes and strive to keep your eyes on the prize . . . that prize is Jesus, the one who loves you unconditionally.

He is everywhere, all at the same time his love goes out to all mankind. Sometimes we come to a cross in the road and we have to make a decision . . . Which way shall we go?

There comes a time in our lives when we reach that turning point, and come to the realization that the things we are doing and the way we are living is more hurtful, stressful, and harder than it would be if we would turn to something more helpful and more of a blessing for us, rather than something hurtful and a curse to us.

May we turn towards something different and better and there is nothing or no one better than God. Therefore, may we turn to God and put our trust in him. God is our refuge and strength, a present help in our times of trouble.

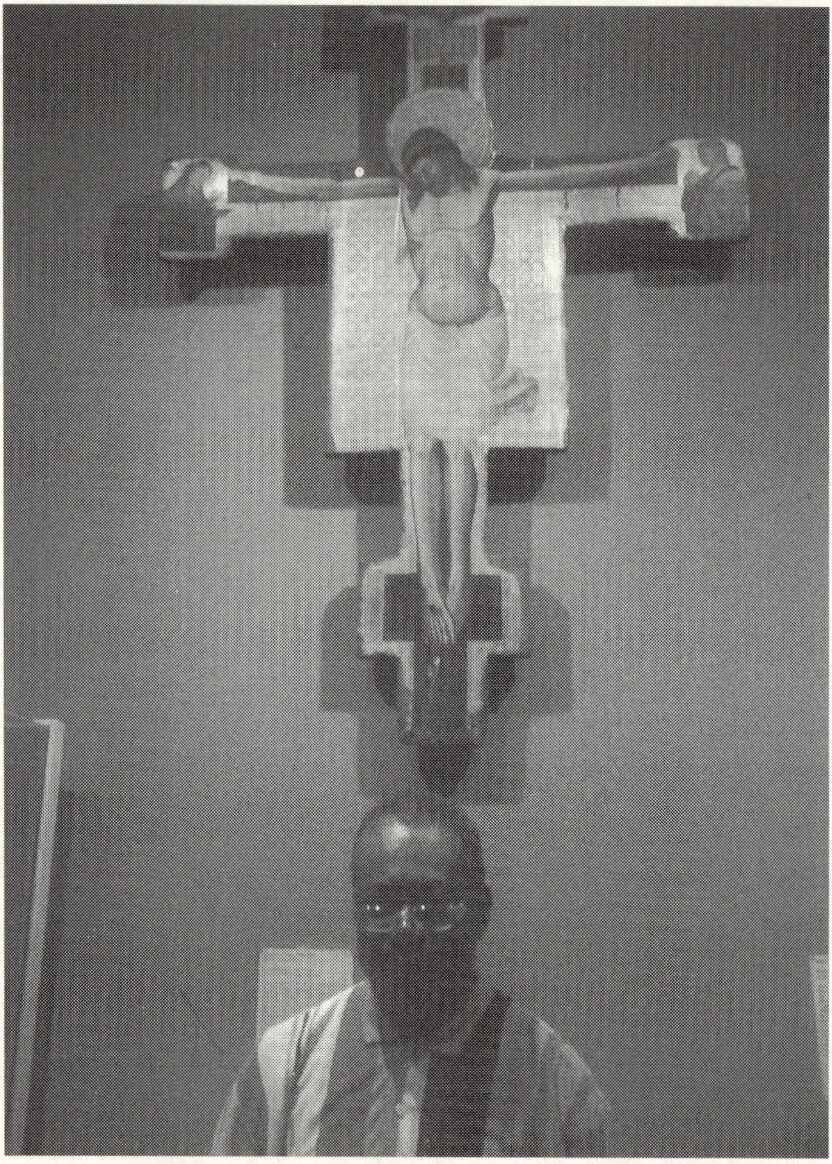

Chapter One

Striving To Stay Focused

(Still missing the mark)

One must go on, right or wrong, whether things are good or bad in your life. One must excel and prevail over our enemy who targets us, to shoot us down daily. He aims to kill us; to take us down for doing our Father's will. Let us continue to strive and stay focused to keep from missing the mark, and to keep the enemy from sticking his fork in us. Because once he sticks his fork in us we are done and he defeats his target. Let us stay focused; keep striving and pressing toward the mark of the high calling of God in Christ Jesus.

Praise the Lord! May ye be found faithful . . . remain in prayer, steadfast, and lead by the Spirit of God.

Let us continue to strive and abide under the shadow of the most highest God. Sometimes our way will get hard and many times things won't go our way. There may even be times when we grow tired and may feel like throwing in the towel. That is the time when one should bow and pray, asking God to give you strength to make it through the rest of the day, and he'll give you strength, mercy and faith, to help you keep striving to run this race.

Jimmy Jordan - The Messenger

To strive one must come alive in Christ, confide in God and He will help you rise above the obstacles placed in front of you, and the adversity that you face from day to day . . . Amen.

When you put forth the tiniest effort to do better, you are striving. When you are helping someone else, that is a form of striving. When you attend church, spending time in worship to God, and fellowshipping with others, you're striving. When you're constantly asking for forgiveness for your wrongs and constantly repenting of your sin, you're striving. Let us stay focused.

Many of us are missing what God is giving us; failing to catch hold of his wisdom, knowledge, and His blessings that follow us.

Let us stay focused and not wallow in our past mistakes and failures. Let us press on and keep our eyes on the prize which is Jesus.

Stay focused on His teachings, and on all of the many things that He has done for us in this life.

Let us stay focused and know we cannot even grow and move forward in life if He doesn't bless us and give us increase for those things we stand in need of.

Let us stay focused and know if it had not been for Jesus, who died for us and lives in us, we would still be lost and we would not be able to live, breathe, or move and do the things we do. Jesus rules supreme! He rules over you, and He rules over me.

He rules over Satan the enemy and He has all power in His hands, yet He is still humble and shows Himself to be friendly.

He is in control. He holds our lives in His hands and we need to stay focused and know we cannot do anything without Him. John 15:5 confirms this . . . and in Jesus' own words, He said, ***"I am the vine, ye are the branches: He that abideth in me, and I in him, the same bringeth forth much fruit: for without me you can do nothing."*** Let us also stay focused on ourselves and focus on correcting our wrongs into rights, and keep reaching for higher heights.

John 15:6 says, ***"If a man abide not in me, he is cast forth as a branch, and is withered; and men gather them, and cast them into the fire and they are burned".*** Many choose not to learn and are burned.

Many of us are missing the mark of the high calling of Jesus; many of us don't even come close to what God is calling us to be. Many of our minds are off track. Many of those who strive to walk upright are off balance, and are constantly falling, missing the mark.

Many of our hearts are out of place, filled with hatred, causing us to miss the mark that He has set in front of us to follow and aim our focus toward His righteousness . . . Amen. Many of us are missing it because we're constantly listening to the enemy, Satan, and we allow him to mislead us, guiding us down the wrong road, causing us to miss what God has waiting for us over on the road of righteousness.

Many of us are missing what God has for us and missing God altogether and all the many blessings He has for us that will bring us joy and happiness.

Many of us misrepresent the heavenly sent one, the son of man that was sent down from heaven, known as the

Jimmy Jordan - The Messenger

King of Kings, Lord of Lords, Prince of Peace, The Bright Morning Star, The Burden Bearer, and a Bridge over Troubled Waters. We need to get this application of love that has been supplied.

Fill in the blanks of the empty spaces in our lives, talk to God about them, and let God use you. He already knows your strength and your weaknesses and what you're able to do.

He knows about the bad things you have done and your desires to seek after righteousness.

I Timothy 6:11-12 reads, ***"But thou, O man of God, flee these things; and follow after righteousness, godliness, faith, love, patience, meekness."*** 1 Timothy 6:12 tells us, **"to fight the good fight of faith, lay hold on eternal life, where unto thou art also called, and hast professed a good profession before many witnesses."** Let us stay focused, O man of God and flee from those things that are not of God and cling to those things that are of God and follow righteousness.

Follow after godliness, keep the faith, lay hold of those things of God and the good teaching you've been taught because those things are eternal those sort of things will stay with you for the rest of your life, until eternity. Keep confessing to be Christ like and walk upright. ***"Philippians 3:13-14 reads, "Brethren, I count not myself to have apprehended, but this one thing I do forgetting those things which are behind, and reaching forth unto those things which are before."*** Amen.
"Philippians 3:14 reads, "I press toward the mark for the prize of the high calling of God in Christ Jesus."
Let us stay focused, keep striving, keep pressing on

right or wrong. Keep coming to God's throne and follow righteousness.

Sometimes we're right; sometimes we're wrong, some days we're right on point. Some days we're dead wrong, far from being right, off track doing our own thing, those are the days when the enemy really targets us, aiming to kill us.

We are the enemy's target whom he aims to destroy. He targets us one by one and shoots us down daily. Very rarely failing to hit and hurt some woman, man, boy or girl, leaving him or her wounded both emotionally, physically, and some spiritually, many are totally consumed unto death.

We are the enemy's target, those who follow after Christ; we're on his hit list. He very rarely misses his target. He hits the majority of those he aims for. Some have escaped, many have been saved; when his aim was off and his timing was bad, causing him to miss the soul he thought he had.

You know the enemy was mad because he missed his target, but God was also glad that his child, and soldier on the battlefield made it home from the war zone.

Many are dead and gone, but those of us who are still here, let us give ear to this word and take heed unto the things we have seen here in the sanctuary and the spoken words that we have heard through our testimonies, singing, teaching and preaching.

Let us keep striving, reaching higher, so when the enemy aims to hit you, he just might miss you because you came up to a higher level in your Christian walk.

Romans 10:14 reads, *"How then shall they call on him in whom they have not believed; and how shall they believe in him whom they have not heard and how shall they hear without a preacher."* Romans 10:15, says, *"And how shall they preach, except they be sent? As it is written, how beautiful are the feet of them that preach the gospel of peace, and bring glad tidings of good things!"*

Let us keep moving closer toward the mark of the high calling of Jesus; the closer we get the easier it will be to hit a little harder to keep from missing it.

2 Corinthians 4:1-5 reads, *"Therefore seeing we have this ministry as we have received mercy, we faint not."* 2 Corinthians 4:2 reads, *"But we have renounce the hidden things of dishonesty not walking in craftiness, nor handling the word of God deceitfully, but by the manifestations of the truth commending ourselves to every man's conscience in the sight of God",* Let us renounce hidden things of dishonesty and walk upright and not in craftiness.

2 Corinthians 4:3 reads, *"But if our gospel be hid it is hid to them that are lost."* Let Christ be known through your voice and the way you walk and talk. Let not Christ be hidden to those who are lost.

2 Corinthians 4:4 reads, *"In whom the God of this world hath blinded the minds of them which believe not, lest the light of glorious gospel of Christ shine unto them."*

Our enemy has blinded the minds of many, Let us stay focused and keep our eyes on the prize.

Corinthians 4:5 reads, *"For we preach not ourselves, but Christ Jesus the Lord; and ourselves your servant for Jesus' sake."*

Preachers that preach God's word do not do it in their own strength and of themselves but through Christ who strengthen them and gives them godly wisdom and knowledge to feed others who are listening and taking heed to His word. How shall they preach, except they are sent? As it is written, how beautiful are the feet of them that preach." 1 Corinthians 15:3 reads, *"For I deliver unto you first of all that which I also received how Christ died for our sins according to the scriptures."* But now Christ has risen from death . . . Amen. Let us strive for a closer walk with Jesus. Let us strive for a greater expectation with no hesitation in fulfilling God's will.

Let us aim to do better and get on point, let us aim to hit it a little harder, and go deeper and further into God's word. For the word tells us that the wages of sin is death. The word also tells us that love covers a multitude of sin.

Who can pay the price of sin if the wages is death? I don't know anyone on earth who can afford to pay the price of sin. But I do know someone who is rich in houses and land and owns all the cattle's on the hill, who is also rich in mercy, overloaded with grace and has tons of forgiveness who will forgive you of all your sins; that someone is Jesus. He has already paid the cost of your sins . . . Amen. Let us keep striving and stay focused.

Jimmy Jordan - The Messenger

I hope you all got something out of this message, called Striving to Stay Focused, (Still missing the mark and the Enemies Target). That concludes this message.

May God bless you; stop listening to the enemy, feeding you lies, causing you to miss the mark. Park your life at God's house and come inside.

Chapter Two

God Spoken Word in Plain View

Praise the Lord, thank God for His word that is spoken in plain view for us to see . . . . When God speaks, people listen; God's spoken word is a token of His love for us, who are lost and broken.

When you hear the voice of God, your mind automatically stops to think and gives Him your undivided attention.

The word that He mentions in this text helps us to reflect on ourselves, so that we may find help in His word to help ourselves.

God's word gives us life.

God's word is spoken and given to those who are chosen and to those whose hearts are cold, frozen with hatred.

God's spoken words give light to help us see better and walk upright.

He has written His word in the hearts of many, and placed it in the minds of those He finds seeking to do His will, and give of themselves in plain view so that others may see God working in them.

It's plain to see the love of God, and His mercy and grace given to us in plain view for the world to see.

It's plain for me to see that Jesus was given to us freely, to save us because God loves us and He knows those who love Him.

Let us not be hearers, but also doers of His spoken word; so that we may detour from wickedness, sin, and disobedience.

It's plain to see God's spoken word was given to help us, not to hurt us; so let us not hurt ourselves by rejecting the knowledge of God's spoken word.

Many of us have heard much of His word, but not enough of it, to keep us from missing it.

We need His word to keep us striving and abiding in His word.

It's plain to see who makes it rain; It's plain to see who came to rescue us when we were lost.

It's plain to see who paid the cost of a debt He did not owe.

It's plain to see who gave His life at Calvary; it's plain to see who picks us up when we are down. It's plain to see who regulated our confused minds.

It's plain to see who healed our hurting hearts.

It's plain to see who woke us up this morning.

It's plain to see that God's spoken word carries power. It's plain to see who keeps us breathing each hour and every minute.

It's plain to see whom we need to call on when we are on our sickbeds.

It's plain to see who we need to call on when we see danger ahead. God's spoken word in plain view is written just for you. God's spoken word talks to our hearts and minds.

He connects with us through the mainline; may we stay connected to Jesus. He's the vine, we are the branches.

1 Thessalonians1: 3 reads, ***"Remembering without ceasing your work of faith, labor of love and patience of hope in our Lord Jesus Christ. Grace be unto you, and peace, from our God, our father, and the Lord Jesus Christ".*** Let us remember all the many times we work faith in our lives, and all the many times we gave our labor of love, even though we might have been going through this or that.

We kept the faith through His spoken word and were given patience and hope. 1Thessalonians 1:4 reads, ***"Knowing, brethren, beloved, your election of God. Many have been called and elected by God."***

May you know that you are loved greatly and God loves to see you doing what He called you to do.

1 Thessalonians 1:5 reads, ***"For our gospel came not to you in word only, but also in power, and in the Holy Ghost, and in much assurance as ye know what manner of men we were among you for your sake."***

As some of you know what matter of men we were and how we behaved, then to see those same men change in plain view, living a righteous life.

May you know it was not just God's spoken word in plain view that changed us, but also His power and Holy Ghost; being assured these men having being changed to live a righteous life for God through His word spoken in plain view. God doesn't change. He stays the same yesterday, today, tomorrow and forever, but He requires us to constantly make changes for the better so that we may walk down the path of righteousness also . . . Amen.

1 Thessalonians 1:6 reads, ***"Ye became followers of us, and the Lord Jesus Christ, having received the word in much affliction, with the joy of the Holy Ghost."***

Many followers of Christ have received His word in much affliction when they were going through many trials and tribulations afflicting them, causing them to be unhappy and full of pain, but God's spoken word is able to give you joy and make you happy in plain view, for the world to see.

1 Thessalonians 1:7 reads, ***"So that, ye were examples to all that believe in Macedonia and Achaia."***

Let us be examples as followers of Christ receiving His word in much affliction, but still holding on knowing God is able to fix the situation.

Keep the faith; keep believing in God's spoken word in plain view.

He speaks to me and He speaks to you. May we all listen and hear what thus **saith** the Lord. His word is given to us to make us wise. His word is given to us to broaden our minds so that we may see the big picture and focus our minds on God's written word that is spoken to us in plain view.

God's word is true, it's not something new. It has been around for years, teaching sinners how to live a righteous life. Come unto Christ, be saved and learn how to behave. We live and learn; as we live, we display God's love. The love of Christ will teach you how to live right. May we learn to turn from the things that are not of God.

God's spoken word speaks to the lost and gives them direction so that they may find their way unto Him.

God's spoken word speaks to our disobedience, so that we may find direction, and correct our wrongs into rights. God's spoken word will convict you and make you aware of what you have been doing wrong. When God is displeased with your actions, He speaks to us.

Hebrews 4:12 tells us, *"The word of God is quick and powerful, and sharper than any double-edged sword, piercing even the dividing asunder of soul and spirit, and of the joints, marrow, and is a discerner of the thoughts and intents of the heart."*

Now that is a powerful spoken word.

God's spoken word will cut you from back to front, His word will cut you coming and going, up and down.

Piercing even to dividing asunder of souls meaning God's word cuts you in parts, in many different parts of your life.

God's word will convict and cut you up. God's word is a discerner of thought.

He knows what's in our minds and the intents of the heart. He knows what we intend on doing before we even commit the act.

He knows our hearts and about everything that flows in our hearts. He knows about the sin within us.

He knows about the issue of life and how the weight of the world falls heavy on our hearts.

If you are broken in pieces, God's spoken word will put you back together in plain view for the world to see.

If you're broken and soaking in misery, God's spoken word will lift you off the pity pot and put you in the spotlight of Christ, and His word will make you right, in plain view for the world to see.

1 John 2:5 reads, ***"But whosoever keepeth his word, in him verily is the love of God perfected, hereby know that we are in him."***

1 John 2:6 reads, ***"He that saith he abideth in him ought himself also to walk even as he walked."***

Many followers of Christ are not keeping God's spoken word, and are far from perfection. We as children of God make too many mistakes and have too many flaws to be perfect, but if we walk even as He walked, we wouldn't make as many mistakes as we do.

If we walk even as He walks, we wouldn't have as many flaws as we do.

Let us strive to keep His word, so that His love may be perfected in our lives. We have a lot of work to do in our Christian walk with Christ.

We all have flaws, but let us pause and look for the cause of these flaws, and when we find them, may we give them all to Jesus and let Him straighten them out . . . Amen.

Chapter Three

Professing to be a Christian and Reluctant to be Obedient

Praise the Lord, praise Him for the good things He has done in your life, and praise Him because He saved you when you were lost. Praise Him for his will and His way.

Many people today are praising the works of the devil, and edifying the bad things that Satan is working in their lives. We have too many people lifting up the work of Satan, and confessing up to his mess, putting him on a pedestal instead of stomping that devil down, and using him as a footstool.

Don't be a fool for the devil and let him continue to use you. Be wise in the eyes of God and use the power that He has given you.

Isaiah 40:29 reads, *"He gives power to the faint and to them that have no might, He increases strength."*

Isaiah 40:30 reads, *"Even the youth shall faint and be weary, and young men shall fall; but they that wait upon the Lord shall renew their strength, they shall mount up with wings as eagles; they shall run and not be weary; they shall walk and not faint."*

God's Spoken Word In Plain View

2 Timothy 1:7-8 reads, *"For God hath not given us the spirit of fear; but of power and of a sound mind. Be not thou therefore ashamed of the testimony of our Lord, nor of me his prisoner, but be thou partakers of the affliction of the gospel according to the power of God."*

We all must take our part in afflictions and suffering, but in doing so, let us do it for Christ knowing that God is able and willing to fix the situation.

2 Timothy 1:9-10 says, *"Who has called us with a holy calling, not according to our works, but according to his own purpose and grace, which was given us in Christ Jesus before the world began; but is now made manifest by the appearing of our savior Jesus Christ, who hath abolished death, and has brought life and immortality to life through the gospel".*

Thank God, for Jesus who abolished death and gave us power to be done with those things that were killing us slowly, and those things that will kill you instantly.

Thank God, for Jesus who bought us life and immortality so that we may live forever in Jesus through the gospel; which is His word that gives life.

His word is a keeper; it will keep you when you don't want to be kept.

His word will keep you when you're striving to help yourself do better.

His word is a *"lamp unto our feet, and a light unto our path",* which will lead us and show us which way to go when we are lost, walking in darkness.

May your steps be ordered in the Lord, so that you may walk upright? Many Christians today are resistant to be obedient to God and reluctant to fulfill His will for their life.

Our lives were designed to bring glory unto God. Let your light shine and live a life that glorifies the father in heaven.

Many people, who profess to be Christians, do not listen and take heed to the teachings being taught. Nor, do they seek after the Lord whole heartedly, many Christians are falling short.

We have countless people confessing to be saved, but are reluctant to behave and obey the word of God, that is written by men who were inspired by God, to pour His wisdom and knowledge in us so that we might be winners over the battle of sin . . . Amen.

Thank God for His wisdom and knowledge that was poured into us to help us grow to be more like Him, and less like them who are sinners of Satan. Let us not be full of lies, faking it until we make it.

Let us be true and wise in the eyes of Jesus.

Let us abide under the hands of the most high and powerful God almighty, so that our lives will be safe and secure in the hands of Jesus. We are protected; our steps are ordered and directed. Walk where He leads you, eat of His word and be full.

Endure hardship, conflicts, and affliction. Trust and obey, do things His way, for the way of the Lord is to be obedient. Follow His ways of righteousness. This message is for all who have been called to walk in righteousness, and to those who profess Christianity, let us listen and be obedient. Let us seek to do His will and not our own; but be more willing to do what He wants us to do; not just things we want and desire.

Jesus spoke a word to us in Matthew 16:24 says, **"If any man will come after me let him deny himself and take up his cross and follow me."**

If we're professing to be Christ like, we're going have to put down some things and deny ourselves of those things that are not Christ-like.

Matthew 16:25 reads, **"For whosoever will save his life, shall lose it; and whosoever will save his life for my sake, shall find it."**

Meaning we are going to have to let go of the things of the *world* to save ourselves from being lost, so that we may be found righteous, walking upright in the sight of Christ.

Matthew 16:26 reads, **"For what is a man profited if he shall gain the whole world and lose his soul?"**

What shall a man give in exchange for his soul? There's nothing on earth that we can compare to having an everlasting life of peace, joy and happiness spent with the father in heaven . . . Amen.

Let us not exchange our soul for the riches of this world and the temporary happiness that comes along with such sorrows, persecutions and pain combined with a mixture of lustful, sinful and disobedient ways; causing professing Christians to misbehave themselves, mistreating Him who covers us with His love. Let us not misrepresent Him who was sent, who lived and died to present life into a dying world.

Many of us, who are professing Christianity, have lost the vision on what it means to be Christ-like.

Many Christians today are missing the mark and are off track, still walking in the dark, constantly falling and losing the fight. If we follow Christ, His word is able to keep us from falling, present us faultless, and strengthen us in the areas where we are weak.

We as Christians and people of the world, need to listen and take heed to the word of God that was written and given to us to help us live and grow, and sow into the kingdom of God by sharing what we know, and giving knowledge to others to help them grow.

Ephesians 2:19 reads, *"Now therefore ye are no more stranger and foreigners, but fellow citizens with the saints and of the household of God"*.

Let us as Christian not become lost, missing the mark of the high calling of Jesus Christ.

He's calling for us to stand, and walk upright; Most of us are falling, lost, walking in the darkness. Many followers of Christ are falling, slipping, and tipping, being tossed around by temptation. 1 John 1:6 reads, *"If we say we have fellowship with him and walk in darkness we lie, and do not tell the truth."*

1 John 1:7 reads, *"But if we walk in the light, as he is in the light we have fellowship with one another, and the blood of Jesus Christ cleanseth us from all sin.*

1 John 1:8 reads, *"If we say we have no sin we deceived ourselves and the truth is not in us."*

1 John 1:9 reads, *"If we confess our sins and repent to God He will cleanse us from all unrighteousness."*

1 John 1:10 reads, *"If we say that we have not sinned, we make him a liar, and his word is not in us."*

1 John 2:4 reads, *"He that saith, I know him and keepeth not his commandments is a liar and the truth is not in him."*

1 John 2:5 reads, *"But whoso keepeth his word, in him verily is the love of God protected; hereby know that we are in him."*

1 John 2:6 reads, *"He that saith abideth in him ought himself also to walk even as he walked."*

1 John 2:7 reads, *"Brethren I write you no new commandment, which ye heard from the beginning."*

The words that are spoken are a token of love, giving unto you to help you walk in a newness. This is the true and living word that you heard that will help you live the life of a Christian.

1 John 2:8 reads, *"Again a new commandment I write unto you, which thing is true in him and in you; because the darkness is past and the true light now shine."*

Many of our dark days are behind us and some of them are ahead of us. God is real and His word is true.

God has spoken.

He has spoken to me and He has spoken to you. Please don't play with Him, because he is not a joke. I sincerely hope that you will get something out of this message.

Professing to be A Christian (Reluctant to Listen and Be Obedient), many of us that are professing Christianity are still missing the mark and walking in darkness.

Let's aim to do better and get on point, and shoot for a closer walk with him, who holds our lives and our future plans in His hands.

Make a stand and stand for Jesus.

He is the reason why we are standing on our two feet.

Get a closer walk with Jesus. He will bless you, help you to do better and become a better Christian, who is willing to listen and do what he wants you to do.

May God bless and keep you.

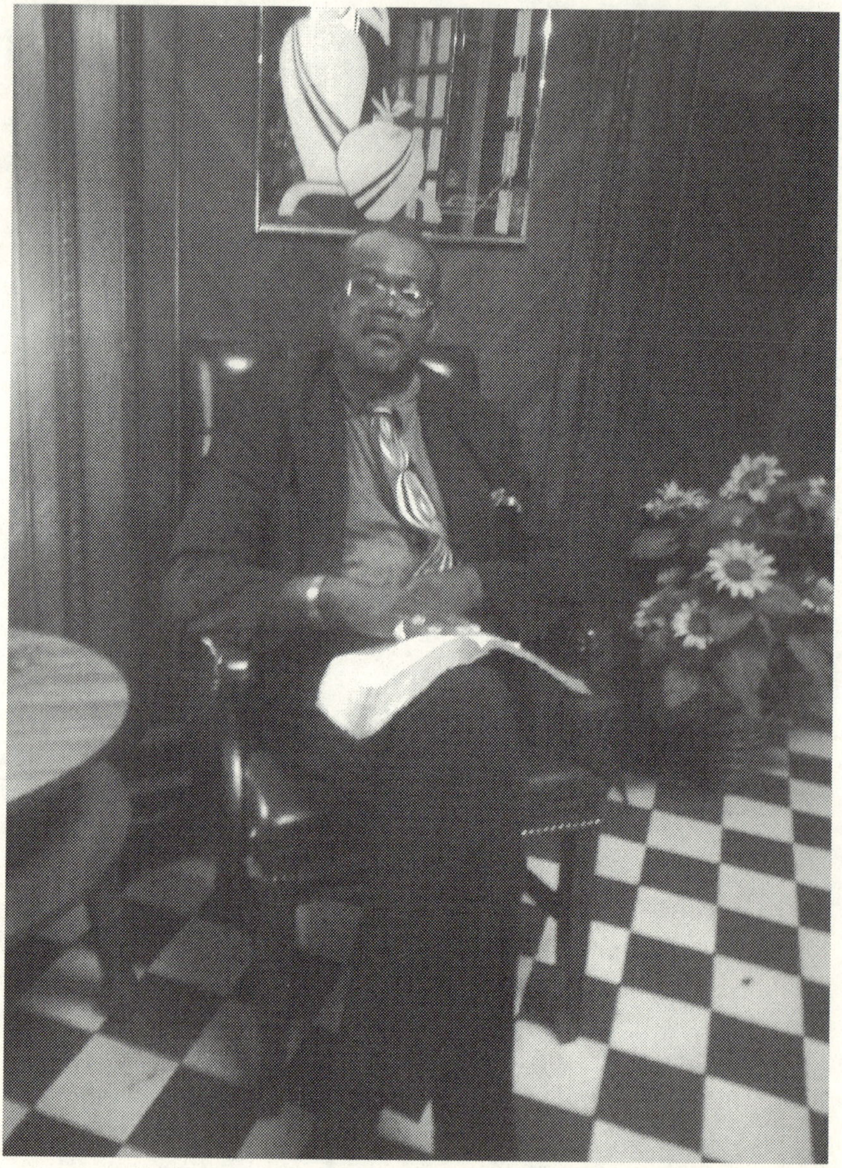

Chapter Four

Walking On the Edge of Life

Help us Lord to walk in this walk without falling as much as we do. Place our feet on a solid rock of that's a sure foundation of Jesus Christ, the rock of my salvation. Help us to stand, give us determination to go on, and do the best we can, striving for perfection.

Let us not walk so close to the edge of life, thriving on doing wrong.

However, if we should happen to fall as we strive to walk up right, let us get back up and come to God's throne right or wrong.

Here's a thought: Let us come to God's throne even when we have done wrong, so that we may receive his mercy and find grace. Read scripture

Psalms 18:1-3.

Praise the Lord, and thank Him for giving us life; thank Him for things being as well as they are.

Many of us are living some dangerous lives, not caring or considering who is in control of our lives.

Many of us live careless and carefree lives, not really considering the things we do and say or how we disobey, grieving God's spirit, leaving Him hurt. God cares for us.

He created us, when we do wrong and reject His word and His love, it grieves His spirit.

God wants us to consider His ways and obey His teaching.

He wants us to love Him and accept Him in our lives; praise Him and glorify His name, and glorify the father in heaven.

He doesn't want us to just think about Him on Sundays, one day a week.

He wants us to serve Him seven days a week without missing a beat.

He serves us with grace seven days a week, by showing us love, allowing our hearts to continuously beat every minute on the hour without missing a beat. God is a good God.

Many of us could be dead and gone, but God let us live on; thank you Jesus.

Many of us take life for granted, because we know God looks out for us, protects us and keeps us safe from any hurt, harm or danger. He gave us the joy of life so that we may live and enjoy our lives, and be happy.

He doesn't want us to be full of stress and strife.

He wants us to be at peace knowing that He is able to calm the storms in our lives. He gave us a choice to choose who we are going to serve. May we live a life that is pleasing to His eyesight. Let us not live our lives on the edge with one foot above ground and one foot in the grave.

That's the same as hearing God's word in one ear and pushing it out of the other. Don't be willing, ready and eager to do the things of Satan. Be willing, ready and eager to do the things of God.

Don't allow yourself to be dead spiritually, unfaithful, unhappy, without understanding of the truth of God's word and all that He is able to do.

Being dead spiritually makes us unable to come alive in Christ. Living on the edge of life is an unpleasing and uneasy lifestyle, unlike God who is very pleasing and easy to live with.

He shows us much love.

He is rich in mercy and loves us unconditionally He goes to war for us and fights our battles, bringing us victory over the enemy.

He stands undefeated and for some unbelievable; let us know for ourselves, believe in our minds, that all things are possible with God.

Many of us today are living our lives on the edge coming close to the end, not knowing just how close we are to the end of our lives, due to our lack of obedience to God's word, slacking in obeying the teaching that has been taught.

We're constantly doing wrong without giving it a second thought; I'm here to tell you, that's walking on the edge of life.

Let us think twice about the decisions we make in life, consider the fall, lest ye slip off the edge, causing the doctor to place some stitches in your head.

It will be almost like Humpty-Dumpty falling off the wall. His life was broken and shattered. Humpty-Dumpty fell and even after the work of the king's horses and men, they were unable to restore him.

The point to this moral lesson is for us to consider our fall, lest we slip and continue to dip in sin, walking on the edge of life. Let us keep our heads up and think before we fall into sin and mess up our chances on making it into heaven.

Let us not be envious of evil doers, follow foolishness, finding ourselves coming up short in lining up with God's word.

Living life on the edge doing our own thing, not listening to what *thus saith the Lord*. Many of us today are running rampant; freely giving in to sin, living on the edge of life with no restraint, no word in our lives to keep us and hold us back; so that we may stand firm and tall.

We fail to hold on to the teaching of God's son Jesus Christ, who strengthen us and keep us from falling.

Psalms 73:1 reads, **"Truly God is good to Israel, even to such as are of a clean heart."**

Many of our hearts are dirty, filled with evil and need to be cleansed.

Psalms 73:2 reads, **"But for me, my feet were almost gone; my steps had well nigh slipped."**

When my feet fell, my mind started to wander and I began to rebel"

Being rebellious caused me to sin.

Psalms 73:3 reads, *"For I was envious at the foolish, when I saw the prosperity of the wicked."*

Many people live glamorous lives, living foolish and doing wicked things. Spending money and having fun investing into worldly things to bring them joy.

They become owners of houses, land, big companies, expensive cars, fine clothing and much more.

Let us invest our minds in Jesus, and not do the things that are wicked and displeasing to God.

Jesus said unto his disciples in Mathew 16:24 *"If any man will come after me, let him deny himself and take up his cross and follow me."*

Meaning we are going to have to put down things in our lives and deny ourselves from accepting all of the filth and garbage the devil pushes our way, presented to us first hand and freely giving to us, deceiving us slowly, stealing our joy and robbing us of our peace.

Matthew 16:25 reads, *"For whosoever will save his life shall loose it; and whosoever will save his life for my sake shall find it."*

If we hold on to the things we love doing, that we know is wrong unto Him who sits high on the throne, then we lose our life in Christ.

If we keep walking close to the edge, we'll lose our life here on earth and slip and fall into the devil's pits.

Matthew 16:26 reads, *"For what is a man's profit if he shall gain the whole world and lose his soul?"*

It profits us nothing, there's no heaven gain, our soul will be lost in the lake of fire, and the only gain would be Satan's gain, another soul to scold in hell because we were walking too close to the edge of life.

We slipped and fell into hell. Matthew 18:8 reads, *"Wherefore if thy hand or thy foot offend thee, cut them off, and cast them from thee; it is better for thee to enter into life halt or maimed rather than having two hands or two feet to be cast in everlasting fire."*

Let us back up from walking so close to the edge of life, before we slip and fall and lose our head. May we get a closer walk with Jesus and go to work for the Lord. Be ye steadfast and unmovable, stand firm holding to the teaching and promises of God.

Do not allow yourself to be tossed to and fro by every wind of doctrine you hear; study God's word, so you will know the truth when you hear it, stand with truth, and the truth will set you free.

The truth of God's word will give you insight on all of the devil's lies.

The truth of God will help you understand the mystery of God and give you knowledge about our Father in heaven.

The truth of God's word will help you do better in life.

The truth of God's word will lead you out of darkness and into the marvelous light.

The truth of God's word will correct you when you're wrong.

God's Spoken Word In Plain View

The truth of God's word is able to pick you up when you're down, and keep you standing and strengthen when your faith is weak.

The truth of God's word will let you see yourself and what you're made of.

It will let you see all of your mistakes, failures and wrong doings.

It will also let you see how strong you can be in Christ.

We are over-comers, more than a conqueror.

God's word said we could do all things through Him who strengthens us.

There's one thing we must do. Stop walking so close to the edge of life.

Stop taking chances on slipping and falling into hell, Stop being enticed to keep sinning.

May we begin to get a closer walk with Jesus . . . God bless you.

You're Messenger Jimmy J.

Chapter Five

Giving Life And Dying at the Same Time

Where would I be if Jesus had not died for me, and set the world free from Sin? I would be lost, tossed to and fro I wouldn't know how to live and love, nor will I know which way to go.

I wouldn't have anyone to show me the way out of darkness into the marvelous light. I would be confused. I wouldn't know anything about the light, if it had not been for Jesus who came into the world as a light and let us see there is a better way in which we can live.

He died and gave us life and instruction on how we should live.

Jesus gave life to a dying world, thank you Jesus for giving us insight.

Thought for today: Jesus is the light of the world in Him there's no darkness, if you need a little light in your life, invite Jesus into your life.
Read Psalms 27:1-4 and Galatians 2:19-20:

"I am crucified with Christ: Nevertheless I live, but Christ liveth in me; and the life, which I now live in the

flesh. I live by faith of the son of God, which loved me and gave himself for me."

Romans 6:5-6 reads, *"For if we have been planted together in the likeness of his death, we shall also be in the likeness of his resurrection. Knowing this, that our old man is crucified with him, that the body of sin might be destroyed, that hence forth we should not serve sin."*

Praise the Lord Saints, and thank Jesus for giving us life.

Jesus Christ walked around giving life to people who were in need of some help, and those who wept from being on the verge of dying.

He went around healing the sick and afflicted, wiping the tears away from those who had been down, lost and in bondage, crying for years.

If you believe and take heed to God's word, His word will set you free. There was a man in the Bible that was blind, Jesus restored his sight with the touch of his hands and said unto him, **"open thine eyes and thou shall see."**

Many of us today are blind; we need a touch from God to open our blinded eyes, so that we can see.

I heard a songwriter say, "I once was blind but now I see." Most of us should be able to relate to this song, from our own wrong doings, and since we are now practicing to do right by God, even though we may fall sometimes and get off track, we get back up and continue to fight because we are striving and practicing to live right.

Jimmy Jordan - The Messenger

I know *I* once was blind. But now I see a better way to live, through Him who restored my sight and my mind, so that I can see. My Bible also tells me about another man whom Jesus spoke a word to and gave life to, a man who was lame, unable to walk. St John 5:2 reads, ***"Now at Jerusalem by the sheep market a pool which called in the Hebrew tongue Bethesda having five porches."***

St John 5:3 reads ***"In these days lay a great multitude of impotent folk, of blind, halt, withered, waiting for the move of the waters."***

St John 5:4 reads, ***"For an angel went down at a certain season into the pool and troubled the water; whosoever then first after the troubling of the waters stepped in was made whole."***

St John 5:5 reads ***"And a certain man was there, which had infirmity thirty and eight years."***

St John 5:6 reads, ***"When Jesus saw him lie and knew he had been now, a long time in that case, he saith unto him wilt thou be made whole?"***

Jesus also sees us and knows our case, and the way we're living short of his word, listening to the devil lie to us. The devil aims to keep us down, making many of us lose our faith in God.

God is real.

He's the same God today as He was back then.

He's real in my life and if you let Him into your heart, He will be real in yours.

Jesus said unto the man at the pool, ***"wilt thou be made whole?"***

St John 5:7 reads, ***"The impotent man answered him Sir, I have no man, when the water is troubled to put me into the pool; but while I am coming another stepped down before me."***

St John 5:8 reads, ***"Jesus said unto him; rise take up thy bed and walk."***

The majorities of us today have legs, but choose not to walk with the Lord. Instead, some of us would rather lay in our mess, constantly saying yes to Satan, when we should be saying, *"No devil, you're not going to keep me bound down!"*

We need to say yes to God. Walk with Jesus and obey His teaching.

We don't need any man to put us in the pool to be made whole.

Today all we need to do is ask God for forgiveness of our sin, and put our faith, and trust in God.

Jesus will make us whole again; Jesus is the way, the truth, and the life.

May our life be hid in Christ that He may be seen so that others may know that we have been washed in His blood, and cleansed through His word.

Therefore, we can give life to a dying world. Many of us today are suffering and dying, hurting and crying, constantly lying unto God and buying the devil's junk.

Let us stop buying what the devil is selling us; instead let us invest our mind and our time in Jesus.

He said in His word, buy of me gold, tried in the fire; God will prove Himself to be real, so that others will know, see and feel that God is real, and alive in your life.

During the times you're being tested, tried and going through the fire, you will still be able to speak life to others, who are down and lost.

God's word will strengthen you and keep you alive when your faith is dying.

Praise the Lord, some people are dying, yet still striving to live for God, even though life may be hard.

Some of us may be struggling and suffering. Sick and barely able to make it, but still have a strong determination to live, to reach out and speak out to help others live, even though they may be dying. That's what the Love of God does for you.

It keeps you trying to do better, helping you and others to go on, right or wrong.

No matter what we're going through on this side, it's all for the glory of God. So we can make it over to the other side, where we won't have to worry anymore about suffering with sickness, and disease, like diabetes, cancer, heart attacks, and all the stings of death.

Once we make it over to that side, where Jesus sits at the right hand of the Father, we won't have to worry anymore about anything, because everything will be better and all is well.

There will be no more crying, no more dying, no more running and no more dark days. Everyday will be sunny and bright, always safe in the arms of Jesus, and living in paradise.

We can enjoy everlasting life in Jesus Christ, riding through the air without care, flapping our wings and listening to the angels sing.

But before we make our entrance there, let us continue to live down here in this mean and cruel world, where people are dying daily, failing to be about God's business and sharing His love.

As we live from day to day, and deal with the cares and affairs of this world, let us help somebody along the way and give him or her life, even though we might be dying. Let us die by trying to introduce someone else to Christ, and then our living won't be in vain.

Jesus gave His life for us, and died on the cross at Calvary, so we might live. He even spoke a word of life unto them who came to kill him, He said, *"Forgive them father for they not know what they do."*

May we forgive others for the things they do. Jesus also spoke a word over this in the book of St John 5:25-28.

He said *"Verily-verily, I say unto you the hour is coming, and now is when the dead shall hear the voice of the son of God; and they that hear shall live."*

St John 5:26 reads, *"For as the father hath life in himself, so hath he given to the son to have life in himself."* St John 5:27 reads, *"And hath giving him authority to execute judgment also, because he is the son of man."*

St John 5:28 reads, *"Marvel not at this; for the hour is coming in which all that are in the graves shall hear his voice."*

St John 5:29 reads, *"And shall come forth, they that have done well unto the resurrection of life; and they that have done evil unto the resurrection of damnation".* Many of us today are living some dead lives,

Spiritually and need to come alive, listen and take heed to the voice of the Lord.

Come forth and stand up, stand for God.

Do good and good will follow you; even when you're down.

Let us speak life to others, so that they may be lifted up.

Many of us are dying spiritually and need to be lifted up spiritually.

Many of us are dying, frying our brains on drugs, and needing someone to speak a word of life unto them, to help them live.

We just heard the word saying they that have done good unto the resurrection of life, and they that have done evil unto resurrection of damnation.

The majority of us already go through enough of damnable things, down here on this side, struggling, straining, paining, and suffering daily physically and mentally.

We don't need to spend our whole life down here going through the fire and then when we make it to the end of our life journey. We will be rewarded with total damnation of hell Fire.

For all the evil and wrong we have done. So let us do better down here on this side and give life to them who are dying.

Let us walk with our heads up even when our spirits are down

Let us not walk in darkness and by the wayside

Let us strive to walk in the light on the solid grounds of that sure foundation of Jesus Christ, continue to walk upright.

Even in our time of trouble, let us help one another, someone is suffering. Someone is hurting, someone is spiritually wounded, someone life is broken.

Someone needs to hear a word of life spoken unto him or her. Because their heart is broken, their home is broken, or their life is broken.

Some of us may very well be the one who's suffering hurting or broken still desiring to give life to others even while we're going through and dying at the same time.

Yet still seeking and trying to save those, which are lost.

Jesus Christ our savior and redeemer looked and saw us, saved us from destruction and gave us life.

May we look and see others who are out here dying and give them life, by leading them to Christ.

Jimmy Jordan - The Messenger

Jesus spoke a word of life through the bible; He spoke to us in 2 Corinthians 12:9 saying, ***"My grace is sufficient for thee; for my strength is made perfect in weakness."***

We can give life to others even when we're down and weak, because he will strengthen us, so we can strengthen others.

May God bless you? Let us give life to someone who may be dying.

                  You're Messenger Jimmy J.

Chapter Six

A New Life

Thought for today: When
The strongholds of life get you down and every time
You try to get up, you fall, Just call on Jesus, he'll
Pick you up.

Praise the Lord Saints, and thank him for giving us a new life with the characteristics of Christ.

We all can be thankful for that new life that God has allowed us to live.

We can all be thankful for things being as well as they are, because they could be a whole lot worse.

Let us be thankful in our minds and hearts, because we could have been dead and gone.

God has been good to us, allowing each of us to have a new start and another chance in life to get it right and live a new life.

Thank you, Jesus, for dying for our sins and forgiving us of wrong doings, so that we can live a new and happy life.

Thank you for giving us a new mind and a new heart. A new love combined with new and righteous thoughts, and new characteristics of Christ.

2 Corinthians 5:17 says, *"Therefore if any man be in Christ, he is a new creature; old things are pass away; behold all things are new."*

God knows that many of us have lived a life portraying the characteristic of Satan. We've been feeding into his evil, deceitful, ways, being led astray day after day into a world of wickedness; evil and wrong doing, full of greed and foolishness.

Some of us are stealing from one another and others killing each other. Most of us have experienced living in a world of envy and hatred.

Let us be mindful of others who are still caught up, and wrapped up in their mess.

W ho are living wrong and displeasing lives unto God? We as the children of God, who are striving live right, let us consider others who also desires to live right and do right, but their hands are tied behind their backs, and their minds are wrapped up and entangled in their wrong doings.

Many are tied to the tribulation, and devastation of this troubled world and their minds are bound down with heaviness from the weight of the world.

They need to be free and I believe their freedom could very well be, inside of you and me, because it was you and me who portrayed the characteristics of Satan.

We displayed those same evil, deceitful, wicked ways. Many of us have had our hands tied behind our backs, with our backs against a wall, and we couldn't do anything for ourselves.

There were times when our minds were bound down with burdens, from the weight of the world, and we needed some help for ourselves.

Jesus Christ who sits high on the throne and looks down below saw that we were in need of his help.

Reached down and helped us.

He lifted our heavy burdens, freed our minds from bondage, and gave us a new mind and a new heart.

He untied our hands so we could reach out and help free someone else who is in bondage.

He gave us a new life so we can tell others about his goodness, so that they may come to believe in him, trust in his word, and continue to spread the gospel throughout the world.

So that we all may become free from whatever it is that keeps a person bound.

God's word is able to free your mind, God reaches down and touches us with his everlasting hands of love, and helps us when we are tied and tangled up in our sin, and our minds are confused and bound down. He freed us and gave us spiritual in sight.

So let us be considerate of others and spread that same love to people who are still lost in a world of sin.

2 Corinthians 4:3 reads, **"But if our gospel be hid, it is hid to them that are lost; in whom the God of this world hath blinded the minds of them which believe not, lest the light of the glorious gospel of Christ who is the image of God; should shine unto them."**

2 Corinthians 4:6 reads, *"For God who commanded the light to shine out of darkness, hath shine in our hearts, to give the light of knowledge of the glory of God in the face of Jesus Christ."*

Praise the Lord Saints, may we as children of God, let our light shine so others will be able to see a way out of living in darkness.

We the children of God could very well be the key to freedom for them who are bound in their minds and locked into sin, and blind to the teachings of God's word.

We the children of God can also be a guide for people who have lost their way in life, by leading them and showing them which way to go. If we lead them to God's word, his word will show them which way to go, and which way not to go.

If you're living that new life, then your life alone can be a guide to the lost, because they will be able to see the power of God through your new life

Seeing, the way he changed you from living that old life could help them.

God is willing and able to help anyone who's in need of some help; anyone who is lost and is in need of a savior, Jesus will help you find your way in life.

Not only that; he'll give you a brand new life.

He will change your old way of thinking to a new and better way of living.

All we have to do is invite God into our hearts and repent of our sins, and he will come in and be a friend until the end.

And fight your battle and help you win the fight.

When you come into the start of living that new life, it almost feels the same as getting a new car.

It will make you feel good and look good. It will make you keep it clean and spotless; it will make you drive with cautions.

It will make you be protective about it and keep watch over it.

It will make you keep up the maintenance on it, and keep it running right.

That's the way we should feel about that new life in Christ, because it was given unto us freely, as a token, as an expression of his love.

It should make you feel better than getting a new car.

A new car is nice to have because it can take you many of places for a long time, it will help make your way in life a little bit easier.

However, that new car won't last forever. When we come into the likeness of Christ, start living, and experience that new life, and new love that comes from above, it will give you new hope.

We can rest of sure that new life can last forever and will last just as long as we want it to.

We also have to be protective of that new life as well.

Let us start by protecting the heart and guard it with a close watch, being mindful of the things we do and say, and evil spirits that will flow into our minds and hearts.

Jimmy Jordan - The Messenger

Let us also keep our minds and hearts clean and spotless as we live this new life, the same way we would keep that new car clean and spotless.

May we polish up on that new life, and keep it shining bright, so that others people who are living in darkness may come to the knowledge of wanting to live right, and live that new life in Christ.

One must also keep up the maintenance of that new life at all cost to keep one's self from being lost.

It's important to maintain and study God's word, the same way we would keep that oil changed in a new car.

We must continue to gain knowledge of God's word to keep our minds and hearts clean, to keep us from living a sluggish, rugged and dirty life.

May we keep up the maintenance on that new life, so we will live a clean and smooth, righteous new life. May God bless you and keep you.

You're Messenger Jimmy J.

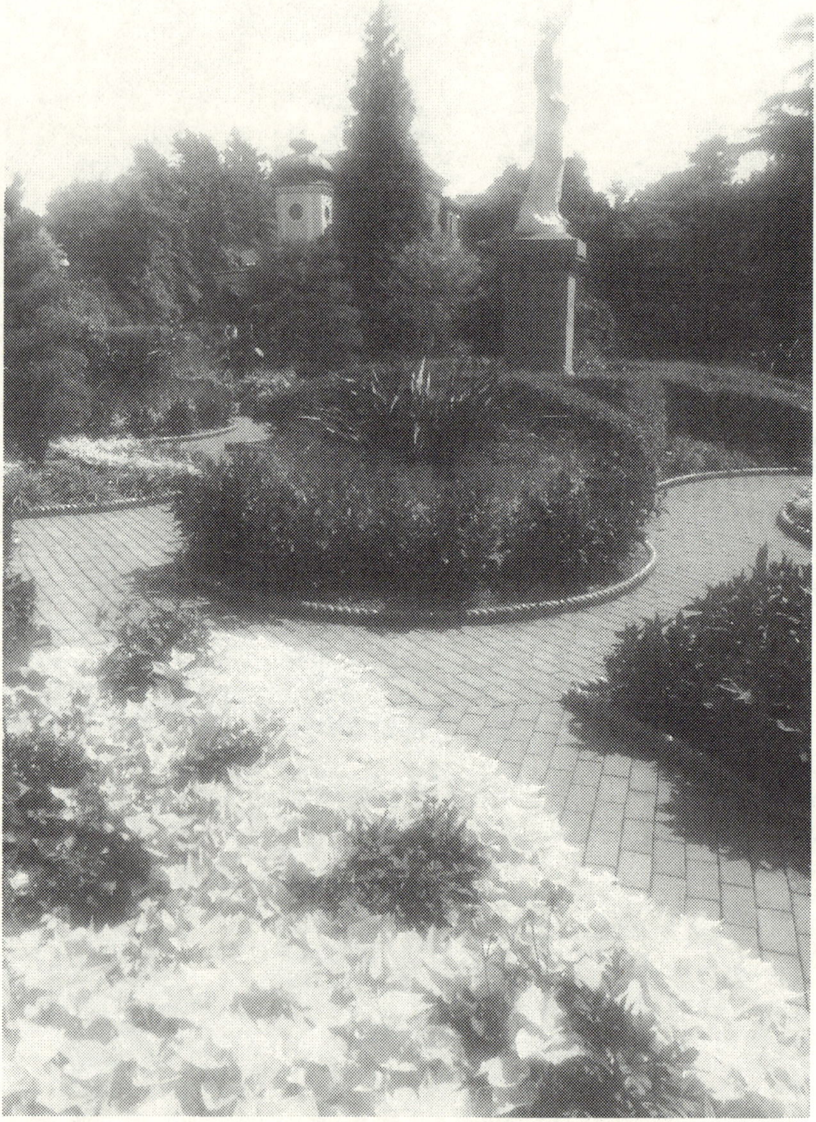

Chapter Seven

Never Knew a Love That Could Do So Many Things

God is a good God, He's been better to us than we been to ourselves. I never knew a love so great. Never knew I would be one of the people God would use to help save the lost, many people of the world today are striving for righteousness and trying diligently to keep it together. Thank God, for the one's striving, but let us be mindful of the many others who are lost, broken vessels whose lives have fallen apart?

Thank God, for Jesus who mends broken hearts, showers us with his love and cleans us up.

Praise the Lord, thank God for the love of Jesus and his love for the world.

Many never knew love could change your direction. Many never knew love is a shield of protection for us. Many never knew that love would take over the wheel when we're driving down the road of destruction, chaos and confusion, and guide us down the road of righteousness over into the land of peace. The love of God will give you peace where confusion used to be. Love has turned many people around from going in the wrong direction and put them on the right path to keep them safe from destruction.

The spirit of love will add peace to your life, erase chaos, and regulate a confused mind.

Many people of the world never knew of this kind of love.

This kind of love will go to war for you.

This kind of love will fight your battle; this kind of love will give you a better mind even after waking up with a bad mind.

This kind of love is rare; this kind of love treats everyone fair.

This kind of love always shows that God cares about you.

Many never knew this love would follow you and go with you to the end of this earth.

Many never knew this love is worth more than gold and any amount of money you could hold.

Even though this love is worth more than gold, it was freely given to men, women, boys and girls, to be told unto other sinners who have waxed cold.

This kind of love is able to penetrate the body, get down on the inside of you, and heal you of any sickness and disease.

This kind of love is able to get into your mind to help you think right and consecrate your thoughts, so your hopes of making it in would not be lost.

Many never knew it was this kind of love that paid the cost of a debt it did not owe.

It was because of Jesus' love for the world he shed his blood and died for you and for me.

Praise the Lord, thank God for Jesus;

It was this kind of love that was sacrificed for all men, women, boys and girls that we may live in a better world.

Many never knew of the pain, agony, sorrows and grief of he who displayed so much love suffer for you and me.

It was this kind of love that held back the hands of the enemy.

It was this kind of love that protected us from any hurt, harm or danger.

It was this kind of love that was poured out into the world to redeem man, woman, boys and girls.

Praise the Lord, for it was this kind of a love that was given to us all from a stranger in the city, who had mercy and pity on those who lived dirty and filthy lives . . . Help us Lord.

God's mercy is renewed every morning and his love is everlasting and breathtaking.

This kind of love will put breath in your body and give you life; this kind of love will also protect you.

Help us Lord to grab a hold of this genuine love that travels to and from the earth, seeking to find those who are lost; It is this kind of love that is a banner over the entire world.

It was the love of a stranger, who walked the earth teaching and preaching about the love of his father. It was this kind of love that prayed for us that we might behave ourselves.

It was this love of a stranger who laid hands on the sick and healed them.

It was the love of this stranger who fed a multitude of hungry lost people. This same love is still feeding us today, both physically and spiritually.

It is this kind of love that is able to put food on our tables when we are not able.

It was the love of baby Jesus who was born in a manger, grew to become man, King of Kings, Lord of Lords, who travel the earth and sail the sea across the world to rescue you and me.

Matthew 24:11 reads, **"Many false prophets shall rise, and deceive many."** Matthew 24:12 reads, **"Tell us and because iniquity shall abound the love of many shall wax cold."**

Verse 11, is very true, yet and still it does not exempt us from being real and digging into God's word for ourselves.

Let us not focus on the shortcoming of someone else, let us keep our eyes on ourselves, so that we might rise higher in our Christian walk.

Matthew 24:12 means that many shall be full of sin because the father of lies has lied to all of us and supplied us with many dirty, sinful thoughts, hoping that one may continue in sin.

It is because of this kind of love that I speak about goes with us and follows us is able to help us withdraw from sin to keep us from engaging ourselves there in.

This causes the lies of the father of lies to backfire in his face, because Jesus came to win lost souls that have wax cold to win us over that we may follow in his footsteps, so that we may be on fire for the Lord also that we may be go to work for Jesus in the vineyard, working hard for the Lord.

Matthew 24:13 reads, *"But he that shall endure unto the end the same shall be saved."*

Hold on, faithful member who follow after Christ, hold on Raquel, keep singing for the Lord.

Hold on Bro. David, keep doing what's right, keep singing to the people, letting them know it may be the last time they do what they do.

It may be the last time I testify about the goodness of the Lord I don't know. It may be my last I deliver his word, I don't know it may be the last time I raise my hand up to the Lord.

I don't know. Brother David, keep singing, let the people know it may be the last time we walk through these doors, I don't know.

Let them know it be the last time we have to come before the Lord, repent and get right with the Lord. Hold on, Min. Dennis Hulsey, stay on fire, and continue to bring the fire of the Lord here and wherever you go that it may heat up the many of lost souls that have wax cold.

Hold on, Pastor Earl Jordan, continue to preach and teach.

Continue to show love to others.

Continue to feed the hungry, and provide shelter for the homeless, continue to walk upright, before the Lord, and continue to stay on the battlefield, seeking to do his will.

I pray every day for strength and forgiveness, because sometimes I get weak, and do wrong.

Therefore, I pray every day that He may strengthen me for the journey, I must take.

Rather we be right or wrong let us come to the throne of grace with repentance; running with hast.

Matthew 24:14 reads, ***"And the gospel, of the kingdom shall be preached in the entire world for a witness unto all nations and then shall the end come."***

One day this love that I speak about is going to come and put an end to all life and everything that creeps on earth; let us begin to wake up spiritually before

We take that long sleep in the night permanently.

Jesus spoke a word to us in Revelations 1:8, saying ***"I am Alpha and Omega, the beginning and the ending,*** *saith the Lord, which is, and which was and which is to come.'*

Jesus came into this world to seek and to save those who are lost.

If you're lost and need some help let Jesus help you. He'll send his angels to find you and help you right where you are.

Jesus is the beginning of our strength; he gives us what we need to make it from day to day.

He's the beginning of our happiness and joy; he's the ending of our troubles, turmoil and sorrows.

He's the beginning of a brighter tomorrow

He came to show us how to live right; he came to give sight to the blind.

He came to teach us how to love one another.

He came to let us know we must forgive each other.

He came to be a blessing, to help us learn how to figure out the lessons of life, and how we must correct our wrongs into rights.

He has succeeded in teaching those who failed in life and help many of us to become successful and do our best during test and trials. Hold on, Jesus will help you, Jesus spoke another word to us in Revelation 1:18 saying, **"I am he that liveth and was dead; behold I am alive** *for evermore . . . Amen; I have the keys of hell and of death."*

Love is the key; Jesus love can keep you out of hell and prevent death.

Many of us are living some hellish lives and death waits at the door, seeking to come inside. Never knew love would prevent death from consuming me.

This kind of love is able to lock and unlock the gates of hell.

This kind of love is able to tell death to go away, come back another day.

Never knew love can do so many things.

Jesus speaks to us again in Revelation 3:19, *"Many as I love, I rebuke and chasten be zealous therefore and repent."*

Revelation 3:20 reads, *"Behold I stand at the door and knock, if any man hear my voice and open the door I will come in to him and sup with him and he with me."*

There's no other love greater than this kind of love, for it was this kind of love that laid down his life for a friend.

For is this kind of love that is able to pick us up when we fall and help us stand over and over again.

I hope you got something out of this message of Never Knew Love Could Do So Many Things . . . May God Bless You.

You're Messenger Jimmy J.

Chapter Eight

Don't Stop, Keep Running
For Jesus Until You Drop

We have many runners and bible thumpers, whom enter this race preparing themselves to come in first place and only a few coaches and trainers to teach and instruct.

The best trainer and coach to help you win this race is the Holy Ghost coach, better known as, *the comforter.*

He'll relax you, teach you, train you, talk to you, walk with you, and run every mile of the race with you to show you which way to go, and lead you to the finish line so you can win with flying colors.

Praise the Lord, thank God for Jesus! Keep moving closer toward him.

Don't stop until you drop.

Many have signed up to run in this race; many have prepared themselves to win this race.

Many have been trained to last, and run to the end.

Many have started out on this journey, but have failed to stay in the race and run with haste.

Don't stop after you have run your first mile. Don't stop when the clouds begin to hang low. Don't stop when your enemy Satan says so. May you say no to the devil, I'm not going to stop, and I'm going to run until I win.

Keep running for Jesus.

Don't stop when the haters start hating on you

Don't stop when you've been lied on and talked about, hold on.

Hold on to your faith. Hold on to the teachings you've been taught, and run on.

Don't stop; keep running for Jesus until you drop.

Psalm 46:9 reads, *"He maketh wars to cease unto the end of the earth; He breaks the bow, and cutteth the spear in sunder; He burneth chariot in the fire."*

He's able to stop the wars from raging in your life. He's able to break the bow that was aimed to shoot you.

He's able to cut the spear from piercing you, relieving you of some serious pain.

He's able to burn down the enemy's camp. 2Thessalonians 5:17-18 reads, *"Pray without ceasing, in everything give thanks for this is the will of God in Christ Jesus concerning you."*

Don't stop praying.

Don't stop believing, don't stop reading His word.

Don't stop teaching His word,

Don't stop reaching for higher heights,

Don't stop serving Him. Don't stop walking upright.

Don't stop knocking on His door.

Keep knocking, He's at home looking through the door watching and waiting to see how bad you really want to come in and how long will you wait on him.

Don't leave from the doorsteps of Jesus, stay with him and His father God . . . . He said in his word, *"I will never leave you, nor forsake you."*

Let us not leave him nor forsake his word. He also said, *"He will leave us peace."*

John 14:27 reads, *"Peace I leave with you. My peace I give unto you; not as the world giveth. Let not your hearts be troubled, neither let it be afraid."*

He said I give unto you not as the world giveth. He said my peace is different. He's talking about that Jesus peace that peace that surpasses all understanding.

He's talking about that peace that's able to regulate a confused mind.

He's talking about that peace that's able to ease the burden of a troubled heart.

Let us run for Jesus and pick up the pace.

Let us run on for Jesus when the enemy is trying to stop us and block us.

May the smoke you leave behind stop him and block him from seeing how you took off and is long gone running with Jesus.

Run on when you're tired and weary.

Run on, when the enemy is trying to make you go astray Remember the race is not giving to the swift, trying to finish in a hurry, but to those who endure to the end.

Let us run on when were being attacked by the enemy from every side.

Let us run on, and don't look back to listen to what the enemy is saying.

Just keep running for Jesus and keep praying.

Continue to stay steadfast, because that is what's going to help you, last until the end and help you overcome the sin in your life.

1 Corinthians 9:23-27 reads, *"And this I do for gospel's sake, that I might be partaker thereof with you. Know ye, not that they which run in a race, run all, but one received the prize. So run that ye may obtain."*

1 Corinthians 9:25 says, *"And every man that strives for the mastery is temperate in all things."*

Now they do it to obtain a corruptible crown, but we are incorruptible.

1 Corinthians 9:26 reads, *"I therefore so run not as uncertainty; so fight not as one that beateth the air."*

We fight not against the air and the wind that we cannot see.

We fight to win and against principalities, powers, rulers of darkness of this world, spiritual wickedness in high places, that we may not see.

But you can feel the blows of Satan and know that something is attacking us with spiritual wickedness, that the time when one should call on Jesus to help you, fight your battles.

He's your helper, protector, redeemer, and your Lord and Savior.

Don't stop keep running for Jesus until you drop!

Isaiah 40:31 reads, **"But they that wait upon the Lord shall renew their strength. They shall mount up with wings as eagles.**

They shall run and not be weary; and they shall walk and not faint."

If at any time one shall fall while running this race, let him wait on the Lord, and if that one call the lord he'll come by, pick you up, and put you back in the race.

He will renew your strength so that you may continue to run on for Jesus.

He gives us his word to encourage us to run on, eat of his word and taste and see that it is good.

He will gives us a drink of his living water that we may never thirst again, to help us run on and win this race.

Many people who drop into the church and sign up to run in this race, have dropped out for many different reasons.

Some drop out because the race was filled with chaos and grief.

Some drop out because other have cheated and set traps to make one lose, playing tricks and games to make you lose the race, so that they may win and see their name come in first place.

Some drop out because they were tired; others drop out because they were disqualified, no longer able to run.

Some drop out because they were unfit and didn't feel that they could make it.

Many were dropped from the race, some had to leave because their names were called from on high and they retired from running in this race.

Many followers are still running for Jesus, keep running don't stop, until you drop.

Some have dropped out because the race was too long and too far away from home.

Some drop out because they never intended on running the distance of this race and doing the duties of a full-time Christian, but a part-time, on-call Christian.

May we ask God to help us become more mature in our Christian walk so that we may become full-time Christians seeking to grow stronger and go deeper into our beliefs in Christ.

Hebrews 12:1-3 reads, *"Wherefore seeing we also are compassed about with so great a cloud of witnesses, let us lay aside every weight and the sin which so easily beset us, and let us run with patience the race that is set before us looking unto Jesus the author and finisher of our faith, who for the joy that was set before him endured the cross, despising the shame, and is set down at the right hand of the throne of God."*

Jimmy Jordan - The Messenger

For consider him that endured such contradictions of sinners against himself, lest we be worried and faint in our minds."

Let us think of how Jesus continues to put up with us and such contradiction of sinners of how so many people fail to deny themselves of the sin in their lives, but prevail in denying Christ in their lives.

This causes so many people to derail the course God has set for their lives and the tracks he has laid down for us to follow; many of us have gone off course.

Many of our minds are off track, but He endured all of our grief, worries, and troubles.

He hung in there until the end and fainted not.

He did not give up; lest we' be worried and faint in our minds.

He went through it all for us.

We are going to have to suffer some things and go through without giving up. One of these days, we're not going to have to worry about running in this race

One of these days, we're not going to have to worry about enduring to the end.

One of these days we're not going to have to worry about studying to show ourselves approved, so that the new you may line up with his word.

God's Spoken Word In Plain View

I heard it's been said that it won't be long. I heard, it's been said one of these days Jesus, is going to come back and crack the sky.

They say the sun is going to drop out of the sky and many people will begin to fry.

I heard it's been said, the dead shall rise first.

1 Thessalonians 4:16 reads, **"For the Lord himself shall descend from heaven with a shout with the voice of the archangel and with the trumpet of God and the dead in Christ shall rise first."**

Matthew 19:30 reads, **"Many that are first shall be last and the last shall be first."**

That's the day we all will drop out of the race to go meet our maker to receive our pay for the deeds done in this body.

One of these days, it's going to be all over.

I heard Deacon David say **"May our good deeds outweigh our bad deeds."**

One of these days we're going to run this race at a slow pace and slide into the finish line to win and ace the tests that are given to us.

Don't stop; keep running for Jesus until you drop . . . Amen.

You're Messenger Jimmy J.

Chapter Nine

Keep the Lights On Listen For My Knock

Many have gone astray, left home; walking around in darkness, living wrong and unpleasing lives in the sight of God.

Many people of the world today are doing their own thing, failing to realize it was God who woke us up this morning and gave us strength to rise up out of the bed.

He gave us our legs to walk with.

He gave us our lives to live unto him.

He gave us our ears to hear.

He gave us our mouths to speak of his love, goodness and the light of Christ that shines so bright.

Praise the Lord, for he's the strength of our lives and the reason why we live. Thank him for being who he is . . . Amen

God has been many different things to us and for us.

He's been a shelter for us.

He's provided a roof over our heads.

He's built a wall of protection all around us.

He's been food for the hungry. He fed us the bread of life and gave us spiritual insight.

He's been a well of refreshing water to a dry and thirsty land.

He's been a hand full of love that has always been there for us to show us that he cares for us.

He's been a rock for us to stand on when we're standing on shaky grounds. He's been a bridge over troubled waters

He's been a peacemaker, when I was lost and couldn't find my way.

He made a way, out of no way. He's been better to us than we have been to ourselves.

He's been a friend to the friendless and a mother to the motherless, a father to the fatherless

He's been our all and all, and we should give him our all and all.

He's going to be the one who's there for us to pick us up when we fall.

Psalm 27:14, reads, ***"Wait on the Lord; be of good courage, and he shall strengthen thine heart."***

Wait I say on the Lord. When we fall, let us wait on him until, he picks us up.

The light of Christ shines upon all of them who are striving to do right and serve him; the light of Christ opens up blinded eyes and let's them see his righteousness and how we should be.

The light of Christ is a lamp unto our feet, and shines deep in dark hearts and empty minds.

Jesus Christ shines his light on our dark and dull understanding.

The light of Christ will find you and reveal to you your wrongs, and the things about yourself that doesn't sit right with God. The light of Christ will point out your sins to you, to let you know there are spots of sin here and a spot of dirt there.

If you continue to do wrong, you become full of sin with dirty spots everywhere. Once the light of Christ has located you, and showed you to yourself; that's when we need to look at ourselves and see we need some help to clean up these dirty spots of sin here and there.

Invite Jesus into your life. He will come in, clean up those dirty spots, and wipe the slate clean.

May God keep shining his light on us? May we keep knocking on the doors of his heart, come on back home unto God and eat of his word, and taste the sweetness of all the good blessings he has in store for you.

Proverbs 10:22-23 reads, *"The blessing of the Lord, it maketh rich and he addeth no sorrow with it."*

It is a sport to a fool to do mischief but a man of understanding hath wisdom. May we put down the foolish things in our lives, wise up and come home. God is keeping the lights on and listening for the knock of that lost child that went astray to come on back home.

Listen for the knock of that one who's broken in spirit and crying on the inside, crying out for some help, looking for the father in heaven to mend their broken hearts and spirit back together to serve as a light living for Christ.

He listens for the knock of that one who lost their way in life, lost their direction and faith in God.

And all those whom lost their respect for themselves and God.

They lost the grip that they had from holding on tight to God. Keep the lights on and listen for the knock of that lost child. Listen for the knock of that one that upholds the truth of your word, knocking on the doors of Jesus looking for more strength and wisdom to carry his word to the lost.

Lord Jesus, may you keep the lights on and listen for the knock of them who are burdened down and heavy laden.

Lord, may you listen to the knock of them running from the enemy, Satan looking for a safe place to hide.

Jesus is our refuge, our safety net, the place we run to for help and protection. Lord, keep the lights on for those shedding tears because their hearts are hurting, filled with anguish and grief, from being defeated by our enemy, Listen for they knock and hear their cry.

Many are knocking on the doors of Jesus and leaving his doorsteps, before they receive the answer to what they are asking for, and before he can give them what he has in store for them.

Wait on the Lord. Matthew 7:7-8 reads, *"Ask and it shall be given you; seek and ye shall find; knock and it shall be opened unto you."* Ask in faith and wait on him to receive your blessing; may you find his blessing through His word. Continue to knock on the doors of His heart and do your part; keep calling on Him until you reach Him.

Knocking on the doors of Jesus gives Him an invitation to come and see about us and knock on the doors of our hearts.

Matthew 13:13 reads, *"Therefore speak I to them in parables, because they seeing see not; and hearing they hear it not, neither do they understand."* Jesus speaks in parables to paint a small picture of moral truth, to teach us a lesson that we might learn from his experience of suffering and dying on the cross for us Relating his suffering to our suffering and light afflictions.

He already showed us how to live.

He shows us how to love and how to give.

We see in the scripture through his word. Although we see not and seem to be blind to His teachings, because we fail to learn and take heed to what He's saying.

Jesus is also saying to many, *hear my word going forth and being taught but they hear not.* Romans 10:14 says, *"How then shall they call on him in whom they have not believed?"*

How shall they believe in him whom they have not heard? How shall they hear without a preacher?"

Many hear the word and hear not, neither do they understand

Many do not understand the seriousness of His word or the power of His word.

The power of His word is able to pull down strong holds; neither do they understand there is life in His word.

Matthew 13:14, *"And in them is fulfilled the prophecy of E-sa'-ias, which saith by hearing ye shall hear, and shall not understand; and seeing ye shall see, and shall not perceive: Which saith by haring ye shall hear, and shall not understand and seeing ye shall see and shall not perceive."* Esaias the prophet already prophesied these sayings?"

Many still fail to hear what the word is saying and fail to see and understand the scripture unfolding right before their eyes.

May God keep the lights on to help you see and understand the scripture and hear what thus said the Lord?

When you're out there in the field being dis-obedient to God's will there's no guarantee you're going to make it back home.

Many of them who left home to go play in the fields are gone on to glory and they never made it back this way again.

We have some out there in the field who's tired of playing and ready to come home that's been playing around on the enemy's territory so long they are lost and their minds are confused, finding it hard to find their way back home.

Someone is lost in the wilderness, roaming around in circles with no purpose, no goals, looking for a way out.

Follow the footsteps of Jesus and he'll lead you out, God sees all and hears the knocks of us all.

He knows about every one of his lost children.

He knows whose scratching to come up higher and those constantly knocking at his door.

Keep knocking and the door will be opened because of your persistence and you stayed on the doorsteps of Jesus, until you got his attention.

Someone is lost in the wilderness, crying, trying to find their way back home saying, "I'm tired, hungry, and lost, I'm coming home.

Someone is lost in the wilderness, seeking for peace and rest.

Someone is lost in the wilderness tired of being used and abused by the enemy, Satan.

Someone is saying, "Keep the lights on, your child that's lost in the wilderness is coming home." John 14:1 reads, **"Let not your heart be troubled; ye believe in God believes also in me."**

Let us put our trust, faith and belief in Jesus; He's the one who's going to come and pick us up out of the mess we're in and bring to his father's house and clean us up."

John 14:2 reads, *"In my father's house, are many mansions; if it were not so I would have told you. I go and prepare a place for you. I will come again and receive you unto myself, that where I am there May ye be also."*

May our works speak for us, and may our gifts make room for us that we may be received by the one whom we believe in.

Jesus has already prepared a place for all of us.

He has the addresses of us all and knows where he's going to place us. However, for all those who are knocking, keep knocking and looking for that glorious gospel of the light of Christ to shines upon you.

King Jesus is keeping the light on for you, so you may see your way unto him.

He's listening for your knock. He heard your cry. He's at home standing by. Watching and waiting for his lost child to come home."

John 10:27 reads, *"My sheep hear my voice and I know them and they follow me."*

John 10:28 reads, *"I give unto them eternal life, and they shall never perish; neither shall any man pluck them out of my hand."*

"John 10:29 states, *"My father which gave them me is greater than all; and no man is able to pluck them out of my father's hand. I and My father are one."*

King Jesus gives eternal life if you make it into my father's house.

You shall live forever.

Keep knocking, trying to get in and die to the sin in your life.

May God bless you, and may you come home unto your father God, eat, rest and be filled with his spirit and receive his best of everything . . . Amen.

                You're Messenger Jimmy J.

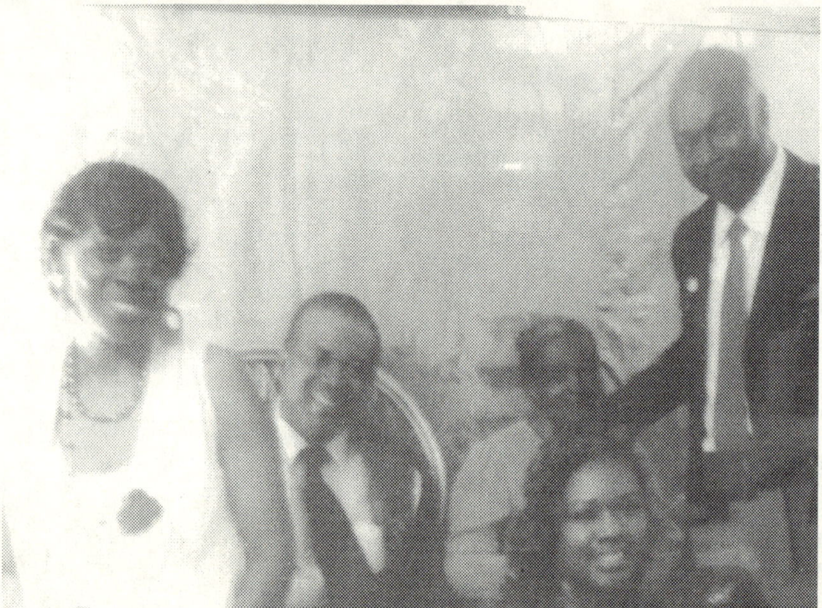

Chapter Ten

Yesterday Is Gone (Tomorrow's Not Promised)

Time is on our side, were living in the last days, we live in a world of greed.

And the days are evil filled with hatred, polluted with wickedness.

Time is ticking and the night is closing in quickly.

Many of our minds have been afflicted from evil, hatred and wickedness.

It's a new day, yesterday is gone, and tomorrow is not promised. We still have time to get it right.

Praise the Lord Saints, God is a good God and he's good all the time.

God gave all of us a choice to choose, in whom were going to serve.

May we choose this new day to serve God almighty?

Who is mighty and powerful enough to pick us all up when we fall?

Strong enough to hold all of us up, when Satan tries to pull us down.

Jimmy Jordan - The Messenger

Each one of us has been wrong, and done things that were displeasing to God. We have wronged him many of times.

The majority of us do wrong every day.

Let us make up our minds to draw the line on doing wrong, while we still have time to get it right, before God draws the line and takes away the function of our minds and all of our time.

Then time will no longer be on our side.

Time will no longer tick for us. The time clock of our lives would stop ticking before we buy our ticket to get aboard that train, that's going to a far better place.

A place where we all would love to stay.

We grieve the Holy Spirit when we do wrong unto God;

We do wrong unto ourselves and hurt ourselves.

Hurt comes in many different ways.

Some are hurting physically, financially, and mentally. Some are hurting from yesterday's sorrows, or the troubles of today.

Many hurting and suffering people need some help.

God is a good God, His love doesn't change,

His goodness remains the same, yesterday, today, tomorrow and forever more.

Yesterday's troubles are over.

It's a new day,

Weeping may last a night, but joy comes in the morning. Thank God, trouble doesn't last always.

Disappointments and the devil torments are only moments that will pass, and can be swiftly turned into moments of today's rejoicing, and tomorrow's happiness.

God is able to fix whatever you may be going through. He's able to turn yesterday's sorrow into tomorrow's happiness and let us see a brighter day ahead.

Praise Him because He's worthy of all praises due unto Him.

I'm here to tell you troubles don't last always.

Nothing stays the same accept God's word.

Everything else will pass. Yesterday is gone; it's a new day,

Tomorrow is not promised to us; Hold on, God knows what we're going through.

Even though we face many of days of hardships, uphill struggles of hard times and battles within our own minds.

He knows the troubles we face day to day

He's the answer to all of our problems.

He's the one who keeps us here from year to year.

Sometimes our hearts may feel fear, but he said in his word "Have no fear, for I shall always be with you."

Sometimes our eyes may shed some tears from grief, misery, and pain.

Many are suffering from the storms in their lives.

Some have been harmed due to the devil's charm.

Troubles of life have rained down on all of us, soaking us with troubles; leaving us drenched in sin. It a new day, yesterday is gone, Tomorrow is not promised, and Yesterday may have been full of failures.

Many of us have failed in our Christian walk.

Many of us are still falling

Yesterday's disappointments, failures, mistakes, heartaches and troubles are gone.

It's a new day filled with new happiness, new hope, new joy, and new chances, to get it right. It's a new day filled with new mercy, new love, and new blessings from God above.

It's a new day, time out for playing.

It's time to get it right with God, by getting his word down in us for real and do better in life.

St John 5:24-25 reads, *"Verily, verily, I say unto you that hears my word and believe in him that sent me, has ever lasting life and shall not come into condemnation; but has passed from death unto life."*

St John 5:25 reads, *"Verily, verily, I say unto you the hour is coming and now is, when the dead shall hear the voice of the son of God, and they that hear shall live"*

We do not have to stay in bondage.

Many people of the world today are in bondage, tied to sin in their lives. Satan has his grips on them keeping them bound; many have found themselves short in lining up with God's word.

All of us have made mistakes and bad decisions in the past.

Let's not live in the past. It's a new day, yesterday is gone and tomorrow is not promised.

As long as the blood still runs warm in your veins, you still have a chance to change.

Times are changing dramatically and so must we.

We must make a change for the better, before things get worse

Tomorrow is not promised and there is no guarantee we are going to make it through the rest of this day. Let's not take life for granted, thinking we're always going to see the next day

Many people made plans for tomorrow. Sad to say, some of those same people died the same day, tomorrow never came to show them a new day.

Let us be thankful for today, even though we face many trials and tribulations from day to day.

Let us stay steadfast, study God's word, stand fast, and be quick to be about God's business, holding on to the doctrine that was given to us, which is his word; His word will last forever.

Troubles are going to come, but troubles won't last always

Tomorrow is not promised to any of us. Tomorrow may be far away.

Today is the day of repentance.

Today is the day we need to be strengthened in and have our spirits fed, so that we may be strong and prepared for battle. Yesterday is gone, it's a new day.

The fight we lost back then was a score for Satan.

God has allowed us another chance to settle the score again to win the fight over sin in our life.

Time is of the essence so let us not wait until tomorrow to do what we can do today. Time is ticking, May we hearken unto the voice of the Lord?

Come to God first and worship him before he comes to you and lets you ride in that hearse, and have you escorted in by some men who will roll you to the front of the church.

Today is the day the Lord has made, let us rejoice and be glad in it.

Romans 8:35-39 reads, *"Who shall separate us from the love of Christ?"*

Shall tribulation or distress, or persecution of famine, or nakedness or peril or sword?

Romans 8:36 reads, *"As it is written for thy sake, we are killed all the day long; we are accounted as sheep for slaughter."*

Romans 8:37 reads, *"Nay in all these we are more than conquerors through him that loved us."*

Romans 8:38 reads, *"For I am persuaded, that neither death nor life, nor angels, nor principalities, nor powers, nor things present, nor things to come."*

Romans 8:39 states, ***"Nor height, nor depth, nor any other creature, shall be able to separate us from the love of God, which is in Christ Jesus our Lord."***

Troubles are going to have their way in our lives, troubles and trials only come to make us strong, not to be weak, resulting in giving up and giving in, and being separated from the love of God.

We are being killed all day long.

This is a very true statement.

We are dying daily and rapidly. We're dying from the rush of lust, to commit sin; many are dying from frying their brains with drugs, nurturing alcoholism, to please the flesh.

Yes, we are killed all the day long. We're dying from sicknesses and diseases. Our days are numbered like sheep for the slaughter. Let us be persuaded, knowing God is able to keep us alive during these dying times and difficult days of trouble.

No matter what comes or goes. Let us continue to stand with Jesus.

He already knows the outcome of these different situations coming into our lives.

Sometimes I wish I could turn the clock back.

I would go back and change many of things, if I could go back and turn back the hands of time, I would turn my whole life around.

Unfortunately, there's no going back in time, yesterday is gone.

Jimmy Jordan - The Messenger

It's a new day; let us use this new day to change some things in our lives, which will turn our whole life around.

Time stands still for no one to turn back the hands of time. We may not be able to go back in time to change some things we did through the year. This new day that has been given to all of us has allowed us to make new choices, new decisions, with a new vision on life that will preserve our time here. To live a little longer, and gain more knowledge of God's word to strengthen us and make us stronger and stronger, time is on our sides, because God woke us up this morning, and gave us another chance to live and grow.

Let us use this new day that God gave us, and make the most of it, by investing our minds and time into our father's business.

It's a good investment!

Our minds will grow, so will God's love Flow from within our hearts, and out of our mouths, without a doubt, you will know that it was the best investment you ever made.

It will prosper you much from spending a little time with God.

You will prosper much more when you invest your mind into our father's business, He will give you more than half the percentage of the business, which is the highest paid profit given to anyone.

Consider when you started out you had no sense, no valuables, no honors, and no loyalty; no love, no hope, no self-respect, for yourself or others.

All you had was another idea, to invest in something real, something good and profitable, something concrete, and something that will stand through the test of time.

You invested your mind into our father's business, and it paid off.

He gave you sense when you had none, He gave you love, when you had none, He gave you hope, He gave you joy.

He gave you life; he gave you everything you were looking for to get out of the deal of investing your mind into something real.

Today is the day to fulfill God's will, today is a day of healing, and today is a day of thanksgiving.

Be thankful for what God has given you and give the same to others

Today is the day to say hello to God and good-bye to that old mess; that messed your mind up and beat you down.

Today is the day to accept Jesus in your hearts; be smart and do your part while the day is at hand, because tomorrow is not promised.

Today is the day to be true.

It's a new day that has been coming since the beginning of time.

It's a special day, set aside just for you, Today is the day to make up in your mind to choose whom you're going to serve because tomorrow is not promised to us.

Who will it be? Satan the destroyer, or Jesus Christ, the savior of the world? Remember time is ticking and you still haven't brought your ticket to make it in, night time is coming; the train to glory is running on schedule.

It will be here soon.

What are you going to do? Are you coming aboard, while there's still room? Come on, get aboard this train and ride down the road of love into the streets of peace over into the land of happiness filled with joy.

Yesterday is gone; it's a new day, tomorrow is not promised.

May God bless you?

You're Messenger Jimmy J.

Chapter Eleven

I Know a Man Who Specializes In Junk

May we give all of the broken pieces of our life unto the man that specializes in junk, along with all of the dirt, hurt and junk that we collect from month to month; so that he may fix everything that is broken, clean up our junk and renew our mind?

It's a good thing to be clean and well dressed, but God looks at the heart, the dirt, and the mess that set us apart from Him.

Isaiah 29:13 reads, *"Wherefore the Lord said, for as much as this people draw near me. With their mouth, and with their lips do honor me, but have removed their hearts far from me, and their fear toward me, is taught by the precepts of men."*

Praise the Lord and give him thanks because he's worthy to be praised.

He's the creator of the world, the maker of our minds, bodies and soul.

If anyone hear among us have any broken pieces in their life, which require some work and need to be fixed.

Jimmy Jordan - The Messenger

I want to let it be known, I know a man who specializes in junk.

He goes around picking up junk, dirty and broken up things that seem to be no good.

He's a working man who goes around emptying trash cans and cloudy minds, filled with grief, misery, and pain, and fills them with love peace, and happiness. He picks up heavy loads of junk, filled will all sort of mess.

He picks up caseloads of broken hearts and mends them back together again. He picks up piles of dirty sin and washes it clean again.

He cleans up dirty and broken things; the reason I know is because he washed me clean and he's still working on cleaning a few spots here and there.

He turns frowns upside down into smiles. He picks up filthy rags, and bags of trash filled with hurt, covered in dirt.

He picks up unpaid bills to those who are behind at the time.

He picks up bow down heads and hungry people starving, wanting to be fed God's word

He will fill you with his spirit unto you say I'm full. He will pick up anything or anyone broken Just so, he can fix it, He loves working with his hands and get junk out of trash cans.

He will even pick you up, if you're down in the dumps. If you're down lost in the trash all around you just look up and reach up, and the man above will show you some love and pick you up.

He will clean you up, fix you up and make you brand new. That's what he does.

He specializes in junk; he takes old and dirty things, cleans them up and makes them brand new.

If you're broken and your heart and mind is, dirty. He will fix you up and give you a clean heart and new mind.

He's able to fix anything or anyone broken and make them whole again, this man never found one thing broken that he couldn't fix or clean. This man found all sort of things and people whom where in the trash, thrown out as junk, Left on the side of the road waiting to be thrown on the garbage truck and crushed. The man I know who specializes in junk came by just in time and saved those valuable things and people from being crushed.

He reached way down in the dumpster and picked them up, saved them from destruction.

He will do the same thing for you and me.

He also kept us safe, and helped us! He saved us from destruction, wept with us, served us. He was beaten and mistreated for us.

He's an innocent man who did nothing wrong, He was just passing by, looked in the trash and found some junk to take home so that he could fix it up, because he's good at renewing junk. I know a man who specializes in junk.

He rebuilds that which has been torn down; He renews the part on the inside that gives you power and the drive to hit it a little harder and goes further following Christ, striving to live right.

Jimmy Jordan - The Messenger

I heard it's been said one man's junk is another man's treasure; this man I know specializes in junk, and place great value on the things we think are nothing.

He places great values on things that are insignificant to us, but are highly valuable to him who hold the broken pieces in his hand.

The same way he holds you and me in his hands.

He kept you for himself; decided he could use you and makes you brand new. He washed you up and cleaned you thoroughly, stripped you clean from your worldly ways. He straightened you out, along with the kinks and bends.

He even took those things balled up deep inside of you, laid them out flat and ironed out their wrinkles. Sprinkled with His blood that justified you and made you clean.

He smoothed out all of the wrinkles and gave you increase, inside and out. He fixed you up, groomed you, and lifted up your head. He regulated your confused mind, and straightened out the minds of those who were programmed to serve Satan.

He converted them over, if you have ever been converted; you know what I'm talking about.

I'm talking about, the power that runs through the mainline. I'm talking about the power that gives you a boost of joy and a full charge of love.

He converted many of us over and placed something down on the inside of us that keeps us striving and reaching higher and higher to be more like Jesus, the one who specializes in junk.

He redirected our minds and the way we think, and hooked it all up to one line that runs from the bottom of our heart to the top of our minds that's connected to the plum line that goes straight up and down from heaven to earth picking up his signals of anyone who plugs into that power, flowing through the main source of power that lights up the entire world.

I know a man that shines light on darkness. I know a man that specializes in junk.

I know a man that will lead you out of darkness into the marvelous light.

His name is Jesus Christ, if you're lost and your life is a wreck, I know a man who will fix it for you free of charge.

The man I know is good at what he does; in fact, he's the best in the business.

He does not only specialize in junk, his specialty is healing broken hearts.

He's a healer and a deliverer, whom is able to heal all of our sicknesses and diseases.

He a faith pleaser; He pleases those who put their trust and faith in him.

He's also known to turn hearts of stone into a hearts of flesh and blood that pumps out real love.

This man I know goes around healing and forgiving the sick, showing love, being about his father's business, healing the sick and afflicted, helping hurting, lost people, cooling down scourging fever and saving those who are lost in the need of some help.

Psalm 107:1-10 reads,

"Give thanks unto the Lord, for he is good. For his mercy endures forever. Let the redeemed of the Lord say so, whom he had redeemed from the hands of the enemy and gather them out from the lands. From the east and from the west, from the north and from the south, they wander in the wilderness in a solitary way; they found no city to dwell in hungry and thirsty their souls cried unto the Lord in their troubles and he delivered them out of their distress; and he led them forth by the right way that they might go to a city of habitation, oh that men would praise the Lord for his goodness and for his wonderful work to the children of men."

For He satisfied the longing soul with goodness, such that sit in darkness and in the shadow of death being bound in affliction and iron; because they rebelled against the word of God and condemned the counsel of the Most High.

Let us not rebel against the counseling of the Most High: instead let us compel our minds and ourselves to the teaching and counseling of His son Jesus Christ

Who said, *"Yet a little while you have the light with you; walk while you have the light."*

He also said *"I counsel thee to buy of me gold, tried in the fire that thou mayest be rich; and white raiment, that thou mayest be clothed and that the shame of thy nakedness do not appear and anoint thy eye with eye salve that thou mayest see, let us open our eyes so we can see what's before us, and not what's behind us."*

Many of us are too busy with our minds entangled in our junk.

I want to let it be known, I know a man who specializes in junk.

Let us put down our junk. This man I know who specializes in junk, has new and better things in store for us.

2 Corinthians 5:17, *"Therefore if any man be in Christ he is a new creature; old things are pass away; behold all things are become new.*

And all things are of God, who has reconciled us unto himself by Jesus Christ and hath giving us the ministry of reconciliation;

Verse18, *"To wit that God was in Christ reconciling the world unto himself, not imputing their trespasses unto them; and has committed unto us the word of reconciliation."*

Praise God, let us have some wits about salvation, and be sensible enough to know God was in Christ. Reconciling the word unto himself and Christ died for the sins of the world, so that we might live and be reconcile back unto him, so as we live from day to day, let us put down our junk that no good and no longer works and pick up the word of God which is very good and works every time.

2 Corinthians 5:20 reads, *"Now then we are the ambassadors for Christ as though God did beseech you by us, we pray you in Christ stead by ye reconciled to God."*

This is He who specializes in junk.

This is He who calms the storms and said *"Peace Be Still"*

This is He who also calms the storms in my life as well as yours.

This is He who parted the red sea so Moses and his people should go free.

This is He who drown the enemy when they came chasing after the people God had set free. This is He who said, *"No weapon formed against you shall prosper."*

This is He who said, *"Follow me."* This is He who said, *"If you have faith of a grain of a mustard seed, you shall be able to move mountains."*

This is He who said; *seek to save those which are lost.*

This is He who carried His own cross, and paid the cost of a debt that He did not owe.

This is He who suffered and bled for you and me.

Jesus died for us.

May we die to some things in our lives that hinder our walk with Christ?

We all have some junk in our lives that we need to let go of.

Galatians 5:7-8 states, *"Ye did run well; who did hinder you that you should not obey. That kind of persuasion does not come from the one who calls you."*

When we are being persuaded to follow after junk, we're not being obedient to the one who called us out of the world of sin.

Instead we're being obedient to the one called the father of lies, who constantly calls us, lying to us about some *junk* he promises us.

Let's stop buying the devil's junk, and listening to his lies! Help us Lord to do better as we continue to strive.

Help us to walk upright. Lord have mercy on all of us.

If anyone plans to make it to see Jesus, let us prepare to go the distance and walk the walk, following the footsteps of Jesus. We have a long way to go to make it to that land far away.

So let us put down our junk, because we're not going to make it to that land, carrying all of our junk.

May we let go and let God help us get rid of the junk in our life

We as Christians carry around too much junk, I know a man who specializes in junk.

I know a man who will clean you up and fix you up; I know a man who will free your mind.

Praise God, I know a man who will look pass your faults and see your needs.

I know a man that will help and give you a better mind.

I know a man that will make your heart glad

I know a man that will turn your sorrows into happiness.

The man that I know turns junk into treasure.

The man I know treasures us, even though we may be full of junk.

May God bless you, you're Messenger Jimmy J.

Chapter Twelve

Redeem With the Precious Blood of Jesus Christ

Sold out for God and to the profession of our faith. On the promise of God sold unto the highest bidder, no one can pay the price that Jesus paid for us. He paid with the nail-scarred hands.

He paid with piercing in his side. He paid with the holes in his feet. He paid with his precious blood for you and me.

Jesus died for you and me, May we die to the sin in our lives for him.

Psalm 19:14 states, "Let the words of my mouth, and the meditation of my heart be acceptable in thy sight."

Praise the Lord, thank God for Jesus and the teaching that he taught. We have been purchased with his blood, we all been bought and paid for with the precious blood of Jesus. We've been adopted into the family of God, clothed with wisdom and strength, dressed in love, walking in faith, let us represent the King of Kings and the things He stands for and believes in.

If He stands for righteousness and truth, let us stand for righteousness and truth.

If He believes in helping others, let us believe in helping one another, and forgiving each other. If King Jesus believes in prayer and trusts in God, let us believe in prayer and put our trust in God. If King Jesus said *"We are more than a conquer."* Let us know and believe that we can conquer anything that comes against us, because he said in his word that no weapon formed against us shall prosper.

He said in his word, *"If I am for you, who can be against you."* Praise God, God is a powerful God, and now that we have been adopted into the family of God, we too are strong and mighty in God.

2 Corinthians 2:9-10 reads, *"Jesus spoke a word, saying my grace is sufficient for thee; for my strength is made perfect in weakness."*

Most gladly therefore will I rather glory in my infirmities that the power of Christ may rest upon me. Therefore I take pleasure in infirmities in reproaches, in necessities for Christ's sake, for when I am weak then I am strong."

When our burdens seem to be too hard to hold and gets too heavy for us to bear, Jesus said give them unto him, and he will carry all of our burdens for us.

God is our strength, when we become weak and fall into the temptation of the devil. Talk to Jesus; ask him to strengthen you in all areas where you are weak.

He will strengthen you, pick you up and help you to continue to run on.

If king Jesus believes in running and not faint, let us run on in spite of what's going on let us not give up.

Jesus lived a life walking upright and being obedient, if we desire to be Christ-Like, let us walk upright and be obedient to what the Lord said.

Ephesians 2:1-3 reads, ***"And you hath he quickened who were dead in trespasses and sins, thank God for Jesus who brought us back to life from being dead in our sin, to be alive in Christ."***

Wherein time past ye walked according to the prince of the power of air, the spirit that now worketh in the children of disobedience.

We all have walked crooked and have been disobedient in some shape, form or fashion.

Among whom also we all had our conversation in times past in the lust of our flesh. Fulfilling the desires of the flesh, and of the mind; and were by nature the children of wrath, even as others.

That at that time ye were without God in the world, but now in Christ Jesus ye who sometimes were afar off are made nigh by the blood of Christ. many of our minds, have been far off from doing the will of God, but through the washing of his blood our minds have been renewed, our hearts have been cleansed and has been made to draw nigh unto God, so that we may have a closer walk with Jesus.

Praise God, there's power in the blood of Jesus Christ.

Even though many of us are drawing nigh to God, many of our minds are still afar off from doing the will of God.

Many things we do are not in his will for us to do. 1 Peter 1:18-19 reads, ***"For as much as ye know that ye were not redeemed with corruptible things as silver and gold.***

From your vain conversation received by tradition from your fathers. But with the precious blood of Christ as of a lamb without blemish and without spot, He purchased us with his life."

He gave his life to save a dying world the least we could do is give up some of the things in our lives that are causing us to die, both physically and spiritually.

King Jesus did not redeem us with corruptible things that would corrupt our minds, body, souls, such as silver and gold; those things that can cause us to have too much pride, thinking too highly of one's self and can cause us to fail.

Some of us think were on top of the world because we possess much silver and gold.

The majority of us care nothing about our souls, thank God for Jesus who redeemed us from our vain conversation of being failures in the world, having no success, made an effort to escape the bondage of failures and layer of corruptions of vain conversation corrupting our minds.

Romans 5:8-10 reads, *"But God commended his love towards us, in that while we were yet sinners."*

Christ died for us, much more then, being now justified by his blood, we shall be saved from wrath through him, for if we were enemies, we were reconciled to God by the death of his son.

Much more being reconciled, we shall be saved by his life.

Psalm 104:5 reads, *"Who redeemed thy life for destruction? Who crowneth thee with loving, kindness and tender mercies? Who satisfied thy mouth with good things, so thy youth is renewed like the eagles?"*

Jesus is our redeemer; He crowned us with love and kindness.

God's tender mercies are renewed every morning, Thank God, for having mercy on us all sending his son Jesus into the world to save us.

To keep us from being lost.

There is power in the blood of Jesus.

There is love in the blood of Jesus, peace and happiness flows in the blood of Jesus.

There's joy in the blood of Jesus, There's life in the blood of Jesus.

There is direction flowing in the blood of Jesus. There's cleansing in the blood of Jesus, He will clean you up, wash you thoroughly and strip you from your worldly ways.

There's healing in the blood of Jesus.

There's forgiveness and healing in the blood of Jesus.

There's protection in the blood of Jesus. The spirit of correction is found in the blood of Jesus

When we go to do wrong and have completed your wrong doings, the spirit of Jesus will come upon you before you do wrong, While you're doing wrong, and when you finish doing wrong, the spirit of God will come upon you, and convict you.

The Holy Spirit let you know that God is not pleased with our wrong doings, being disobedient, and constantly failing to please God.

There's compassion and understanding in the blood of Jesus, the blood of Jesus flows through the minds of all of his people and teaches them the truth

He opens up blinded eyes.

He lets us know about all the ways of the world and what lies ahead of us, trust and believe in God and the son of man and you shall succeed and be victorious in life.

It's the blood that keeps us alive from day to day.

I heard some ask others, "Do your heart pump blood or Kool-aid?"

We know that the heart pumps blood, but the question is, are you strong or weak? If your heart pumps blood let us be strong and stand up for God.

For if it pumps Kool-aid, you'll lie down and be weak unto the devil! Hypothetically speaking, every one of us have disobeyed and in a moment of weakness, we dishonor God; falling short, unable to hold fast to his word. We've been unable to keep the commandments of God true and working in our life.

We find ourselves unable to keep the promises we've made to the Lord.

King Jesus is our strength when we're weak; he said in his word, *my grace is sufficient for thee.*

Everything we've done and said unto him, who sits high on the throne, has already been nailed to the cross.

All of our dishonesty, disobedience, craftiness and overflowing of sin that rains in our lives, it's all under the blood of Christ.

Jesus bore our sins and was bruised for our iniquity; the chastisement of our peace was upon him and with his stripes, we were healed.

We are like sheep that have gone astray; we have turned to our own way and the Lord hath on him the iniquity of us all; it's all under the blood.

Thank God for Jesus our Lord and savior, who came to seek those that are lost.

Lost sheep going astray, likewise many have been found and saved unto Christ.

Let us not continue in wrong doing, but let us continue to walk upright seeing, that all of our sin is under the blood.

Let us be filled with the spirit of Jesus who will lift us above all of our down falls, shortcomings and failures.

He brings us through the devastation of sorrow and every giving temptation, trust and depends on him.

He will lead us into a brighter tomorrow; he will go with you and stand by you.

He will give you the strength you need for today to help you stand.

May we pray to God for the things we need and want He will give you your heart's desire and supply all of your needs?

Thank you Jesus for redeeming the world and reconciling us back unto your father God and unto yourself the son of man.

Titus 2:11-14 reads, **"For the grace of God, that bringeth salvation hath appeared unto all men;**

teaching us that denying ungodliness and worldly lust we should live soberly, righteously and Godly in this present world."

Looking for that blessed hope, and glorious appearing of thou, great God and our savior, Jesus Christ.

Who gave himself for us so that he might redeem us from all iniquity and purify unto himself a peculiar people, zealous of good works?"

People, like me and you, who have a strong zeal to live for God and the son of man. 1 Peter 2:9 reads, *"But ye are a chosen generation, a royal priesthood, a holy nation, a peculiar people; that ye should shrew forth the praises of him unto the marvelous light."*

Job 19:25 reads, *"For I know that my redeemer lives and that he shall stand at the latter day upon earth."*

I know he lives because he lives in me and helps me stand when trials and tribulations have overwhelmed me and the weight of the world is on my back, making me about to fall for the devil's schemes; Jesus gives me the strength I need to help me stand and he redeems me once again.

What He does for me, He'll do the same for you, because that's what He does.

He is the redeemer and restorer, He saves and restores broken, lost, hurting people, and with His precious blood, He paid for our sin, He gave his life.

Thank God for Jesus. May God bless you?

You're Messenger Jimmy J.

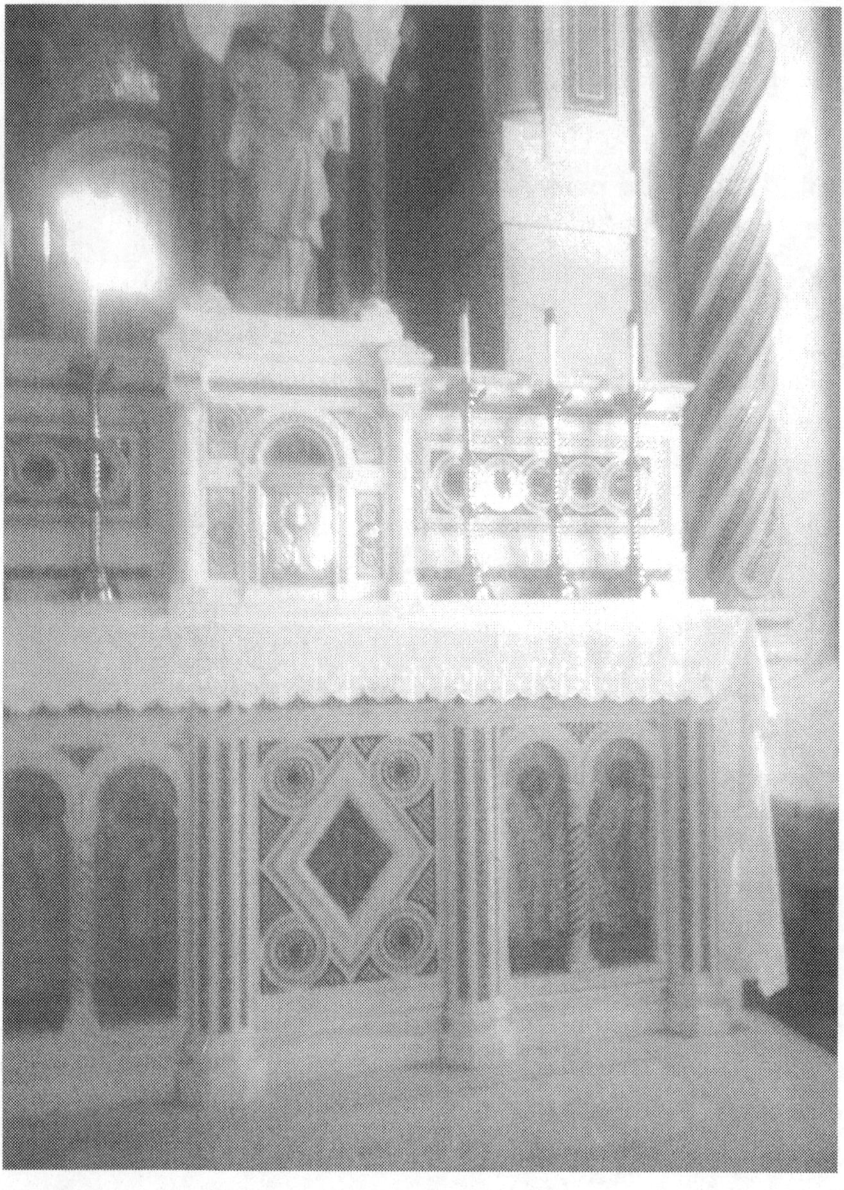

Chapter Thirteen

Rise Above the Flood

Thanks to God, who watches over us day and night, protects us and keeps us safe.

God brought us safely through the storm and the rain that brought about a flood in our lives; leaving us to drown, swimming in sin and drowning in lust.

Thanks to God who lifted us above the floods in our lives.

I know He lifted me above the floods of hell and high waters.

He placed my feet on the ground where I now stand on a solid rock, that rock is Jesus.

Praise the Lord Saints; thank Him for picking us up out of the muck and miry clay, shaping us, molding us and making us to be what He's calling for us to be.

God has brought many of us out of darkness into the marvelous light.

He lifted us above the floods and is still lifting us above the floods of hell and high waters. Surrounded by filth and garbage, floating in contaminated waters, flooded with snakes and sharks ready to eat us and swallow us alive.

Even though we are in the midst of snakes, sharks, and different people with evil spirits like angry beast.

God is able to put a cease to the things that are ungodly, overwhelming your mind and over powering you from time to time.

Let us remember that God the creator of the world is more powerful than any human being or creature that He created, and He's able to protect you and keep you safe from any hurt, harm or danger that may come your way.

God is able to lift you above the floods of hell and high waters.

When the waters get too deep to stand in, and much too dirty and dangerous to swim under it.

God will keep you when you can't keep yourself.

Many people have lost their lives in a flood.

I'm here to let it be known God is able to save you, and raise you above the floods of muddy water and sinking sand. Place your feet upon a rock, that rock is Jesus, who is able to keep you, sustain you, and raise you above the floods.

His word will carry you over the high tides of failure in life and help you to succeed and do better in life.

His word will bring you over the rough waves of trouble creeping into your life.

Even though, the storms of life have rained down on all of us and filled us with grief, misery and pain from the floods of life.

God is able to save us by raising us above the floods.

Many of us have flooded our lives with sin.

Many of us were sinking in sin and some of us are still dipping in sin, slipping in our Christian walk.

There have been times in our lives when we all have slipped on the road of righteousness and fell into sin, allowing our flesh and lustful desires have their way repeatedly.

Help us Lord, to stop dipping and slipping.

If it doesn't apply to you, let it fly, Many of us flood our minds with different things, we cling to thinking it's a way out and a way to help us get over our troubles, Jesus is the only way of escape.

He's the only one who can bring you over troubled waters and raise you above the floods.

Many of times, we go to God for forgiveness and repent of our sins and without a doubt.

He will forgive us, bring us out, and give us a second chance to get right.

He said in His word, He will toss our sins in the sea of forgetfulness and remember them no more.

Many of us are flooded with temptation and bad imaginations.

Times are hard and the days we're living in are evil, a crooked and perverse nation, filled with hatred, flooding each generation, but God is able to raise us above the floods.

Many of us have flooded our hearts with hate, hating one another, let us not hate instead show love and flood the world with love instead of hate.

Many of us have flooded our minds with negativity, but the love of God will change you from living a negative life to living a positive life.

Many people's houses and land have been destroyed in floods.

Many of valuable things have been washed away, destroyed and lost. Let us not be lost and destroyed from the floods, rising in our lives.

Thank God for Jesus, who sits high on the throne, came to redeem the lost and give us back everything that was lost.

He's our savior, He could also be called the lifeguard of the world, where the people are swimming in sin and drowning in lust.

Jesus has many names, because He is loved by many.

He said in His word, I'll be whatever you want me to be. Some call Him Master; some call Him the Prince of Peace.

Some call Him the Alpha and Omega.

He's the beginning and the end.

He's the King of Kings and Lord of Lords. He's peace in the midst of a storm.

He's a bridge over troubled water; He'll raise you above the floods in your life.

Some call Him the bright morning star; some call Him in the midnight hour

Some call Him father, because He's a father to the fatherless and friend to the friendless.

He's our strength when we're weak; He's bread to a starving land.

He's God almighty; He's the man with the master plan, who holds the world in His hands.

He'll pick you up when you're down, He's our burden barer.

He is a way maker, when it seems we just can't make it.

He'll make a way for us; He will bring you over and help us to stand.

He said in His word, He'll never leave us nor forsake us. God is real, His love is here to stay and His Holy Spirit will always be around.

May we as Christians stay around the church and let his spirit abide in us as we continue to strive.

Hold on, stay strong.

God will raise you above the floods in your, life many of us are drowning in debt.

Most of us owe more than we're able to pay, some of us are even drowning in sorrows.

I'm here to tell you, God is able to lift you above the floods, and bring you into a brighter tomorrow.

He'll give you joy, even when times are hard He will still bring you joy.

If your spirits are down; He'll pick you up and lift you above the floods of depression, rejection, and recession. Our world is in a recession and, businesses are reducing.

Many people were losing their jobs due to that recession.

But God is able to raise us above the floods of life and rebuild our world again. He will build businesses back up to help the people survive and bring joy and laughter to all those who are drowning and depressed in this mess our world is in.

2 Chronicles 7:14 reads, *"If my people which are called by my name shall humble themselves and pray, seek my face and turn from their wicked ways, then I will hear from heaven and will forgive their sins and heal their land."*

May we seek God's face and pray for a healing in the land and in our own homes and hearts, so that He may raise us above the floods in our lives.

When you're striving to do right and live right, the Lord Jesus Christ will be by your side to help you rise above the floods.

Isaiah 40:28 reads, *"Hast thou not known, hast thou not heard, that the everlasting God, the Lord, the creator of the world of the ends of the earth, fainted not, neither is weary, there is no searching of his understanding."*

He knows all about our troubles, He heard our cry.

He felt the tears of those weeping and those on bended knees.

He heard our plea and He will answer the prayers of those who are sincere and righteous. God is not a God that He should worry, even though the rain may pour and the winds may blow and the clouds may hang low.

Have no fear; put your trust in God; When the waters get high and you feel like you're about to drown, fear not, sometimes we put ourselves over in the deep and have a hard time swimming our way out of it, even though the winds may blow and the rain may pour, and the clouds may hang low, have no fear

Put your trust in God and believe in His word.

Luke 6:46-49 reads, *"And why call me Lord and do not the things I say, Whosoever cometh to me and heareth my saying and doeth them I show you to whom he is like; He is like a man which built an house and digged deep and laid a foundation, on a rock: but he that heareth and do it not is like a man that without a foundation built an house upon the earth against which the streams did beat vehemently and immediate it fell and the ruins of that house was great."*

Mark 4:37-39 reads, *"And there arose a great storm of wind and the waves beat unto the ship so that it was now full. He was in the hinder part of the ship asleep that was Jesus in the back of the ship sleep on a pillow; and he arose, rebuked the winds, and said unto the sea peace be still and the wind ceased, and there was a great calm; and he said unto them why are ye so fearful? How is it that ye have no faith?"*

God is able to calm the storm that we face day to day and save us from the flood rising in our lives.

We too must call on Jesus, the same way they did, saying Lord, Lord, with a loud voice, saying Master, Master, come see about me. I need you now. I'm sinking fast, Save Me. Wait on the Lord and he'll come to your rescue and see about you.

He may not come when you want him, but he'll come right on time, and lift you above the floods of hell and high water.

God is also a warrior; He said, *"I'll fight your battles."*

Exodus 15:6-10 reads, **"Thy right hand O Lord hath become glorious in power; thou right hand O Lord hath dashed in pieces the enemy and in the greatness of thine Excellency thou hast overthrown them that rose up against thee. Thou sent forth thy wrath, which consumed them as stubble."**

Meaning He ends their life, **"And with the blast of thy nostrils the waters were gathered together, the flood stood upright as a heap of the sea."**

The enemy said, *"I would pursue I will overtake, I will divide the spoil.*

My lust shall be satisfied upon them. I will draw my sword, my hand shall destroy them."

And, God almighty turned things around, drowned the enemy thy didst blow with thy wind the sea covered them they sank as lead in the mighty waters.

God is almighty and powerful who will raise you above the floods but for the ungodly and wicked enemy who tries to rise against him. He'll also drown you in the flood. May God bless you?

You're Messenger

Chapter Fourteen

The Burden Bearer

Matthew 11:28 & 30 reads, *"Come unto me, all ye that labor and are heavy laden, and I will give you rest, for my yoke is easy, and my burden is light."*

Praise the Lord Saint, thank God for being a problem solver, who is able to solve any problem; big or small.

When you are down in spirits and life challenges and disappointments make your heart feel sad, remember it's only for a short period, because trouble don't last always. If you want to feel good like a Christian should.

Talk to Jesus He will lift your spirits and make your heart glad

That is why He left His Holy Spirit here, to comfort us and be our guide, so that we could call on Him in our times of trouble.

When you feel like you're being treated unfair, call on Jesus and tell Him about your problems.

You can call on Jesus anytime of the day for any reason, even in the midnight hour.

He will listen to your cares and concerns he already knows your cares and fears.

He's watching all of us through each year.

God even knows when we're crying, because He can feel our tears, He also knows the people who have put forth as an effort in trying to make it.

He knows the ones dying in their sins; whose chances are slim to none on making it in to receive that crown of righteousness for the victory they could have won, and hear our father in heaven say well done.

Many of us sometimes wonder if and how we're going to make it and hear those words from the Father in heaven say, **"Well done Thou good and faithful servants."**

Many of us often wonder how we're going to make it, even down here in everyday life, living from day to day.

Sometimes the road gets rough and times become hard and tough to deal with on a daily basis.

Some say Lord have mercy, give me strength, and help me make it through the day and that's the way many of us make it through the day, we call on the Lord. God will give us the strength we need, to make it through the day, plus some extra to help us face another day.

Some of us get tired of carrying the heavy load, and all the bags troubles, with grief.

Many of us get tired of carrying the weight from day to day and need a relief.

Well I'm here to tell you that Jesus is your relief and your burden bearer.

He said in His word to cast all of our cares on Him and He would lift our burdens. His yoke is easy and His burdens are light. Cast all of your cares on Him and He will give you rest.

He will make the rough edges smooth and your hard and tough times easier and your day will be filled with joy. You will have peace in the mind to help you get through the rough and hard times, He will regulate your mind from being confused and make your mind think right, so that you will be able to do right.

He'll give you the strength and power you need to win the fight against the battle of sin.

But even though the enemy Satan may show up in your life, trying to win you over to a place of misery, suffering and pain, I want to let you know you can win that battle, by staying focused and keeping your mind on things that are of God.

Many of us are dying in this battle of life and from the sin within.

Fighting the battle of sin may look like you're fighting a losing battle, but that's just what the devil wants us to think, so that he can keep beating on us.

Hitting us with all kinds of blows, trying to hurt us, and knock us out until he gets to that ultimate goal, which is to drop us and leave us lying flat out cold.

Nevertheless, for now as long as we are still standing, he will be punching and beatings us; almost knocking us out leaving us dazed, walking around stumbling and falling from all of the punches and blows Satan has snuck in on us. Some of us can barely see the road and don't know which way to go.

If you want to win this battle against sin, keep fighting even if sin is winning you over, and beating you down.

Keep fighting because the battle is not over, as long as you're still standing, you have a chance to turn this fight around and stomp the devil under your feet, because he is defeated and sin no longer winning you over.

The victory is yours, because Jesus won that battle a long time ago and His victory still stands today.

If we want to be winners in this battle of sin, we must continue to pray and resist the devil and his ways.

There are many people lying up dying from all the slaps and punches, gunshot wounds that the devil has afflicted upon them.

Many of us are alive physically, but dead spiritually with no mind to praise God, or to give thanks for the things he has done.

Most of us have hands, but don't use them to reach out and help someone else.

Many of us have hands and fingers that work well, but won't pick up a bible and read God's words for ourselves, which makes us spiritually dead.

Many of us have legs and feet to walk with, but we still find ourselves falling as we try to walk right, and live a Christ-like life.

All of us have a heart, but many of us have no love, which makes us spiritually dead, God gave each one of us a heart so that we may live and love.

Thou shall love the Lord thy God with all thine heart and with all thy soul and all thy might.

We also are to love our enemies and bless those who use you. Count your blessings and you won't have much room left for your troubles.

I read over in God's word St John 14:1, ***"Let not your heart be troubled; ye believe in God, believe also in me."***

Referring to his son Jesus, remember troubles don't last always, because God is a heart fixer.

He can fix anything that you might be going through. He's able to fix it and make your heart glad.

Because He's the burden bearer and the problem solver, He won't put any more on you than you can bear.

He said in his word, for us to cast all of our cares on him and He will carry our burdens, Jesus is the answer to all of our problems.

    May God bless you. You're Messenger Jimmy J.

Chapter Fifteen

Salvation is free

Praise the Lord thank God for Jesus!

Here we are again coming together on another day; by the grace of God. Through the salvation of the Lord I find it to be an honor and a privilege to be able to provide you with a positive message.

As we come together in God's grace, truly, it's His grace and mercy that continuously saves us. Through the salvation of the Lord, although salvation is free, we must pay the price that is going to cost us to keep it and stay free. May you take heed to God's word, which is able to save your soul and make you whole.

Stay focused; keep your eyes on the prize. That prize is Jesus.

Psalm 118:14 reads, ***"The Lord is my strength and song, and is become my salvation."***

Praise the Lord Saints; thank Him for His love, mercy and His amazing saving grace.

Because truly it was grace that allows us to run in this race. It's a very fast-paced race, filled with cheaters, liars and dangerous people who don't play the game fair.

These people are out to beat us and don't care what they have to do to hold us back, slow us down or knock us off track and make us lose our focus.

The race is not giving to the swift but to those that endure to the end.

God's word said, "We are to be quick to listen and slow to speak.

Let us be quick to take heed to God's word and quick to obey his teachings and run from destruction, we know disobedience causes destruction.

Let us be more constructive to obedience rather than destroying our lives and corrupting our minds although salvation is free, it's going to cost us to keep it and hold out until the end.

It's going to cost us some so-called friends and so called fun. We must continue to run on for Jesus and stop engaging in some of the pleasure of this world.

It's going to cost us to give up many pleasures of this world; it's going to cost us to give up the wrong for the right, although we live in this world.

We are not of this world; We can't live and do the same things as people of the world 1 Peter 2:9 reads, *"But ye are a chosen generation, a royal priesthood, an holy nation, a peculiar people: that ye should shew forth the praises of him who hath called you out of darkness into his marvelous light."* Amen.

Let us strive to walk in that light although salvation is free, it's going to cost us to walk upright, before the Lord Jesus Christ and God almighty.

Who give us our strength to stand and walk right or wrong? Let us be careful of the way we walk because he can easily take away that strength and we won't be walking wrong or right.

We'll be lying on our backs, so be careful of the way you walk because the way you walk could cost you your life.

The same way it has cost many others who have failed to walk upright.

1 Peter 2:11 reads, *"Dearly beloved I beseech you as strangers and pilgrims abstain from fleshly lust, which war against the soul."*

Jesus will give you power to fight any battle that wars against the soul.

Jesus died on Calvary and gave salvation to all men; so that we all may be free from sin, although salvation is free, we must pay the price that it's going to cost us to stay free.

Philippians 2:12 reads, *"Wherefore my beloved as ye have always obeyed not as in my presents only now much more in my absents, work out your own salvation with fear and trembling."*

Philippians 12:13 reads, *"For it is God which working in you both to will and do of his good pleasure."*

Philippians 12:14 reads, *"Do all things without murmuring and disputing."*

Philippians 12:15 reads, *"That ye may be blameless and harmless, the son of God without rebuke in the midst of a crooked and preserved nation among whom ye shine as lights of the world."*

Let us count the cost of the wages of sin and the time we spend giving our minds and lives over to Satan.

Let us strive to do better and begin to give our minds over to Jesus, so that we may live a better and more pleasing lifestyle unto God.

We all have room for improvement, because none of us are perfect. We all have done wrong, but God is a just God.

He forgives us for all of our wrongs, because He's a God of love and forgiveness.

He's full of mercy and grace;

He's a God of peace and understanding he understands and knows that people in the world are lost, living in a crooked and perverse nation, a generation of curses.

From our fore fathers whom many of them lived and died in sin.

Polluting the world with lust, fornication, envy, jealousy, evil spirits, murders, rapist, truth breakers, hypocrites, falser find the truth.

And many of disobedient people disobeying God's word.
God the father understands that we were born into sin.

When we first entered into this lost and dying world from a baby, from our first words and from our first steps.
We were stepping and into a lost and dying world and our first sights were looking upon unrighteous people.

We were smothered in sin, before we even got a chance to live.

That's why He sent His son Jesus to die for our sins, so that we may live.

When He died, He set the world free from sin, and brought salvation unto all men.

Praise the Lord, thank you Jesus for saving a sinner like me, and many of other sinners whom changed their lives and the way they live through God's word.

Speaking of those who carry God's word and minister God's word unto all who have an ear to hear it.

Jesus died for us upon an old rugged cross and shed His blood for the lost, which gave salvation unto all men.

Salvation is free; the salvation of the Lord is upon us, because He died for us and set us free.

Praise the Lord; the salvation of the Lord is also upon you.

When He died for me, He died for you and the rest of the world too.

So that we all may be free from sin!

May we as Christians die daily to the sins that are within our lives.

Have a life that's pleasing in God's eyesight, so that we may shine bright as the children of God; walking in the light that have been redeemed and set free by the salvation of the Lord.

Psalm 62:1-8 reads, *"Truly my soul waiteth upon God; from Him cometh my salvation. He is my rock and my salvation; He is my defense. I shall not be greatly moved. How long will ye imagine mischief against a man? Ye shall be slain all of you; as a bowling wall shall ye be, and as a tattering fence.*

They only consult to cast him down from his Excellency; they delight in lies; they bless with their mouth, but curse inwardly.

My soul waits thou only on God; for my expectation is from him.

He is my rock and my salvation; He is my defense. I shall not be moved. In God is my salvation and my glory; the rock of my strength and my refuge is in God."

Trust in him at all times; ye people, pour out your hearts before Him. God is a refuge for us.

He's who we can run to for help He's our safety net in times of troubles.

God is a mighty and powerful God Who will protect you and keep you safe with his everlasting arms of protection; He has kept me safe down through the years and protected me repeatedly from many dangerous situations and difficult times

Luke 3:3-6 reads, ***"And he came into all of the country about Jordan, preaching the baptism of repentance for the remission of sins; as it is written by Esaias the prophets saying the voice of one crying in the wilderness, prepare ye the way of the Lord; make his path straight."***

Every valley shall be filled and every mountain and hill shall be brought low and the crooked shall be made straight, and the rough ways shall be made smooth."

We all have walk through the valley of the shadow of death and been down through the valley of sorrow and death and sat in the seat of despair; all flesh shall see the salvation of God. May God bless you?

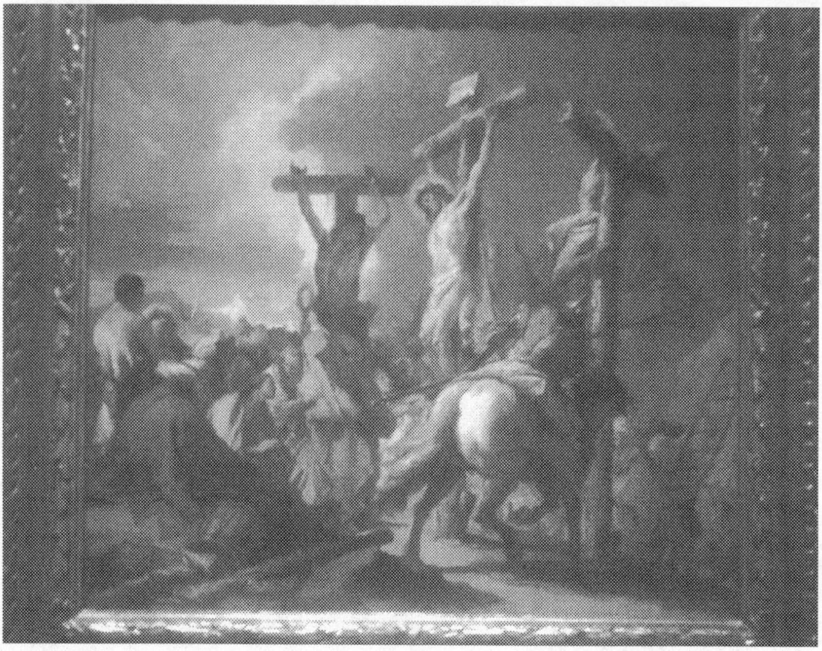

Chapter Sixteen

Victimized by Devices

Praise the Lord and thank Him for things being as well as they are, because they could be a whole lot **worst**.

The vast majority of us here today are victimized by some sort of dilemma or device that has a grip on their life. We the children of God are victim of Satan, who target us and tries to destroy us by shooting us down every day, victimizing us with his devices.

Satan is slick and conniving, he doesn't always hath to kill us by the hand gun, many times he uses us, the victim, to use our own hands to kill ourselves, sad to say but it's true, many people of the world today are killing their own selves and dying by self destruction.

From devices we ourselves clamp a hold of and hold ourselves back from moving forward, he don't always hath to use other people to destroy us, many people are dying by self destruction.

And keeping themselves bound to this, and bound to that, many of us are bound and tied to sin.

We've done many things to ourselves, victimized and tied to the sin in our life.

Jesus died for our sins on Calvary He set the captive free, anything that's not of God and has captured your mind, you can be free from it through God's spoken word in Jesus name.

Thank God for Jesus who gives us second chances over and over again.

Many of us are victims and many of us have been slain from the slander of Satan falsifying the truth into a lie, constantly lying to you and playing with your mind, telling you things to discourage you.

But Jesus constantly sends people to speak a word of encouragement to us, to keep us striving. So let us go on, right or wrong and let that devil know you are a child of God.

Even though we may be victimized by his devices, let us be persuaded and know God is able to give you power over the devil's devices.

And pick up your lowered head, we as children of God have the victory of a victorious God and the son of man working in our life.

Making us more than conqueror's over those things that come to bring us down.

We all have trials and tribulations, persecutions and afflictions, many of the children of God are afflicted and guilty of not keeping the commandments of God as well as the promises they made unto him.

One day we will have a trial date set face to face with God to plead our case, when you are asked all the many different question why did you behave this way and why did you behave that way, may you speak truthfully and say sorry Lord for the things I've done that were wrong, but I was victimized. This world is full of the devil's devices clamping hold of us, holding us down from arriving to our destiny, in climbing to a higher level in our Christian walk.

Webster tells me that a vice is a evil conduct or a habit, a moral fault, or weakness. Many of us are guilty of conducting ourselves in an ungodly fashion, clinging to ungodly habits, which is a device the devil uses to keep us bound and confused.

May we strive to do better because we know better.

The word moral means to tell right from wrong. Moral fault means we knew better when we were doing wrong.

But we sometimes allow ourselves to do things wrong and displeasing to God Almighty, because of a moment of weakness.

Many of us are weak to the devil's devices, the moments of weakness that are shown from us engaging in doing wrong are stored up in the den of Satan, strengthening him to become stronger and stronger, our weakness is his strength.

If we do not want to make that devil stronger, then we the children of God must stop being weak, careless, and free hearted to his followers.

Close the door of your hearts to Satan, stop letting him take up space rent free.

May you open the doors of your hearts to God and the son of man; who will come into your hearts and fill the empty space of your heart and minds.

He's a mind regulator and a heart fixer, He will regulate your mind so you can think right, He'll fix's your hearts so you can love right, He'll see to your needs and look beyond your faults and give you the desires of your hearts.

Romans 10:10 reads, *"For with the heart man believeth unto righteousness and with the mouth confession is made unto salvation."*

Romans 10:11 reads, *"For there is no difference between the Jew and the Greek; for the same lord is over all is rich to all who call on him."*

Romans 10:13 reads, *"For whosoever shall call upon the name of the Lord shall be saved."*

Verse 14 states, *"How then shall they call on him of whom they have not believed and how shall they believe in him they have not heard and how they hear without a preacher."*

May we who have ears to hear listen and take heed to what thus said the Lord.

Many of us have been criticized, talk about, beat down, and thrown outdoors like a piece of trash.

Many are the afflictions of the righteous. Thank God for Jesus who is a healer and a deliver, whom has deliver many people from self afflicted wounds.

Jesus has soothed many hurting hearts. Isaiah 53:4 reads, **"Surely he hath borne our grief and carried our sorrows; yet we did esteem him stricken, smitten, of God and afflicted."**

Romans 53:5 read, **"But he was bruised for our iniquities; the chastisement of our peace was upon him; and with his strip we were healed."**

This world is full of sinful people lost and dying, crying out for some help, from the hurt and pain of self afflicted wounds.

Jesus said in His word, *come unto me all ye that are heavy laden cast your cares on me, and our give you rest.*

When the storm of life is raining down troubles, and troubles begin knocking at your door, creeping into your house, flooding the floors that are waxed with peace are now stained with troubles.

When the floods of trouble are raining in your life, call on Jesus. He'll cease the storm of troubles and give you peace in a world of confusion.

When you get stuck in life and it seems like you're not able to move forward or backwards sometimes you may feel like you're not sure if you're coming or going. Stand still and see the salvation of the Lord move on you and pick you up out of whatever ditch that may have you stuck.

Look to the hills which cometh your help Jesus is on top of the mountain of troubles; call on Him and He will come and see about you.

Isaiah 63:8 tells us, *"Surely they are my people, children that will not lie; so He was their savior."*

Verse 63:9 shines the light on the goodness of Christ. Verse 9 reads, *"In all their afflictions he was afflicted, and angels of presence saved them, in his love and in his pity he redeemed them and bared them and carried them all the days of old."*

Thank God for Jesus who had pity on our lives and was sympathetic on holding back some punishments that are due to me and you.

He looks beyond our faults and failures, and saw our needs and blessed us with the things we stand in need of. He gives us our hearts desire. Even though many of us do things that displease him; grieving his Holy Spirit, while victimization is attacking your imagination.

Many of us never get tired of been victimized by the devil's devices. We criticize one another not realizing when we hurt each other with assaults and attacks, we also bring hurt and afflictions to the son of man better known as Jesus Christ, the King of Kings and Lord of Lords.

Who already died for our transgression and our iniquities' was afflicted up on him for the chastisement of our peace.

He died so we can live.

May you stop letting the devils devices hold you back from moving forward Amen,

May God bless you.

                You're Messenger Jimmy J.

Chapter Seventeen

He Changed Me

Time brings about a change in everyone's life; time is an historical period that comes from a historical God.

Time is a period doing which an action is processed, we as children of God and people of the world are processed daily of a series of actions, and motions leading to a process of manufacturing us daily giving us time to change.

Thought for today: Change and turn from your wicked ways. He changed me. Praise the lord, and I give thanks unto him because He worthy.

He who sits high on the throne and sees all of our wrong doings is God Almighty, and the son man knows and understands. He knows our struggles, hurts and pain. Many are struggling on a daily basis, many are hurting and crying, dying from the beat down of a mean cruel world filled with unfair people. They're dying spiritually and physically from senseless killing. None of us can prevent death. When the death angel has come and parked at your door entered your house to pick you, up must be prepared to take your ride over on the other side.

He knows and understands all of our faults and failures; that's why he gives us time to change over and over again. Let us strive to change our wrongs into rights.

I've been wrong many times, many of the things I used to do I don't do anymore. Many places I used to go, I don't go there anymore.

He changed the way I think, he changed the way I look. He even changed the way I eat and sleep, he changed my diet to keep me around here a little longer. He changed my restless nights into peaceful nights of sleep.

The shoes I use to wear on the wrong feet have been changed to the right feet.

The souls of the shoes that I wear now have been made to last from everlasting to everlasting.

I can walk this walk much better than before now that my shoes are on the right feet because of him who changed me and gave me the mind to put my shoes on the right feet.

God regulated my mind to think righteous thoughts so I can walk upright.

Even though many stumbling blocks are put in my way, He who is able to remove the stumbling blocks out of our way is able to make our pathway straight and clear.

He removed negativity out of my ears and has allowed me to hear positive thoughts; He will do the same thing for you.

May you allow him to change you from living a negative life to a positive life. Give him a chance to enhance your thought pattern; may you let his teaching lead you and be your guidance. Change is not always easy to do, but when you change for the better it will always make things better for you and the people around you, nothing stays the same except God's word.

May God Bless you, your Messenger Jimmy J.

Chapter Eighteen

Displaying More Determination and Less Frustration

Many people in the world today are frustrated and tied down with burdens, afflictions, conflicts, persecutions and stupidity, which causes one to display frustration. Webster tells me frustration means to prevent from carrying out a purpose. Sometimes we lose our focus on the important things that really matter and become unfocused and frustrated over things that do not mean anything of importance.

Let us be more determined to focus on things that really matter in life. God did not allow His frustration to put an end to us when we were living negative and wasteful lives, instead he allowed his son Jesus to die for our sin.

He gave us life; power from on high and strength to go on even when we are face with heavy burdens, tests, trials, and living in poverty follow by hatred, crime and racism. Even in this day and time; though we face bad times of sorrows and frustration, let us display more determination to go on and face tomorrow, looking to the author and finisher of our faith to carry us through each day.

2 Timothy 4:3-6 reads, ***"For a time will come when they will not endure sound doctrine but rather their own lust shall they heap to themselves teacher having itching ears."***

That time has made its arrival here. People do not want to listen to God's spoken word, but rather do their own thing and lust after one another. There are many people dead and gone that could have still been here if they would have listened to God's spoken word.

May you take heed to the words you read? Verse 4 reads, ***"And they shall turn away ears from the truth and turn to fables."***

Verse 5 says, ***"But watch thou in all things endure afflictions do the work of a evangelist, make full proof of thy ministry I am now ready to be offer and the time of my departure is at hand."***

Paul was ready to take his flight and depart from this wicked world of sin, let us prepare ourselves and get ready to take our flight to that land far away.

Because one day we too are going to depart from this world of sin but until then let us display more determination and less frustration.

Paul fought the good fight of faith, he finished the course. We're still on the battlefield fighting everyday warring against our enemy Satan. Many others are trying to survive and stay alive in Christ, let us be more determine to live a life like Christ, and then we will be less frustrated.

Many people of the world today are frustrated and in bound with burdens, afflictions, and conflicts persecutions and stupidity; which causes one to display frustrations. Let us be more determined t o focus on things that really matter in life.

Praise the lord and thank God He did not allow His frustration to put an end to us when we were living negative and wasteful lives. Instead He allowed His son Jesus to die for our sins.

When he died He gave us life, power from on high and strength to go on, even when faced with heavy burden, tests and trials and living in poverty, follow by hatred, crime and racism.

Even in this day and time, even though we face bad times of sorrows and frustrations, let us display more determination to go on and face tomorrow looking to the author and finisher of our faith to carry us through each day.

We must constantly fight to walk upright and live like Christ, being determined to live for Christ can take you a long way with less frustration. When one is determine to live for Satan it can take you down a bumpy road full of pot holes, chaos, confusion, negativity, and unforgiveness, fast! You're bound to crash and wreck your life, causing you more and more frustration, leaving you devastated and frustrated.

Satan comes to devastate your life with wrong doing, evil and bad thoughts. That's how the enemy creeps into your life and ruin good Godly thoughts that have been successfully placed there by God almighty.

Giving thought to the devil only tears down what God has already built up. Therefore let us not give thought to the devil and his devices but let us give thought to God's spoken word and strive to keep our minds on Christ.

Philippians 2:5 says "Let this mind be in you which was also in Christ Jesus." Amen.

Phil. 4:7, *"And the peace of God which passes all understanding shall keep your hearts and minds through Christ Jesus."*

Verse 8 says, *"Finally brethren whatsoever things are lovely, whatsoever things are of a good report; if there be any virtue and if there be any praise, think on these things."*

Determination keeps our wheel turning, determination keeps our fire burning, determination keeps you moving toward that which you're determine to do. May we be doers of God spoken word.

Determination means coming to a decision or the decision is reached, it means to be firm. Let us all stand firm and have a made up mind, firm in our thinking,

God's Spoken Word In Plain View

fixed on living for Jesus. Determination means to be free from doubt, not weak or uncertain.

Determination is used on both sides of the fence; Satan uses determination as an offense to God and the son of man and all his followers to bring them down. Satan is determined to keep lying to you, determined to make you fall and constantly trip you up. He's determined to confuse your mind, because he is the father of lies, lying is what he do best. But getting you to believe his lie is what helps him to get you to live that lie. He's determined to hurt you and **laugh at you** when you cry.

He's determined to see you die and watch you fry! We're just a portion of the season in the pie. He doesn't want to just taste the pie; he wants the whole pie in the sky.

He's determined to bring down all of God's children, but as long we, the children of God stay connected to Jesus Christ, we can make it.

Study to show yourself approve that you may line up with his word.

He will help us in the areas where we need help. St. John 15:4 tell us to, ***"Abide in me and I in you. As the branch cannot bear fruit of itself, except it abide in the vine"***

We cannot bear fruit, except we stay connected to the vine, if a branch is disconnected and cut off, the fruit of that branch will not grow, nor will we as children of God grow spiritually if we disconnect ourselves from God and the son of man.

In verse 5 Jesus tells us in his own words saying, *"I am the vine ye are the branches; He that abide in me and I in him. The same bring'eth forth much fruit; for without me ye can do nothing."*

Being without Jesus is like a fish trying to swim without water. On dry ground that fish will soon die, just like we would be spiritually dead without Christ in our life.

Without Christ we can do nothing, not a thing. Without Christ we wouldn't be able to walk, talk, move, or breathe; but because of Jesus Christ who reigns supreme, with Him we can do all things.

Philippians 4:13 reads, *"I can do all things through Christ which strengthen me."*

It's his strength that carries us every day. Without him we wouldn't even have a day. We would be lost in total darkness; we do not have to be lost in darkness because Jesus died for all who were lost.

He came into the world as a light. He came to shine the light on those living in darkness; I can truly say I'm glad the light of Christ shined on my life.

St. John 1:1 tells us, *"In the beginning was the word and the word was with God."*

Verse 2 *"The same was in beginning with God."* Verse 3-4 reads, *"All things were made by him; and without*

him was not anything made that was made. In him was life; and the life was the light of men."

Verse 5 reads, ***"And the light shiniest in darkness; and darkness comprehended it not."***

People all over the world need to display more determination and less frustration.

Many people in the world, from all walks of life are walking down the road of uncertainty and unforgiveness; living unintelligent and unfruitful lives. Unable to produce the seed of Christ in someone's life.

Many people of the world today are uncertain about who they want to live for, God or the devil.

If you don't mind the chaos and confusion of evil doers who bring death, pain, misery, sorrows, destruction choose the devil. He corrupts your mind so you can live a confused and troubled life, filled with bad spirits seducing you out of your dignity and determination, leaving you sad and frustrated. Satan keeps you walking down the road of uncertainty and unforgiveness living an unpleasant life. But if you desire to live a pleasant life, full of opportunity and possibility, filled with peace, happiness and hope for the future, may you choose to live a Christian life.

Jesus will help you stay determined so you can continue to walk down the path of righteousness,

Amen. You're Messenger Jimmy J.

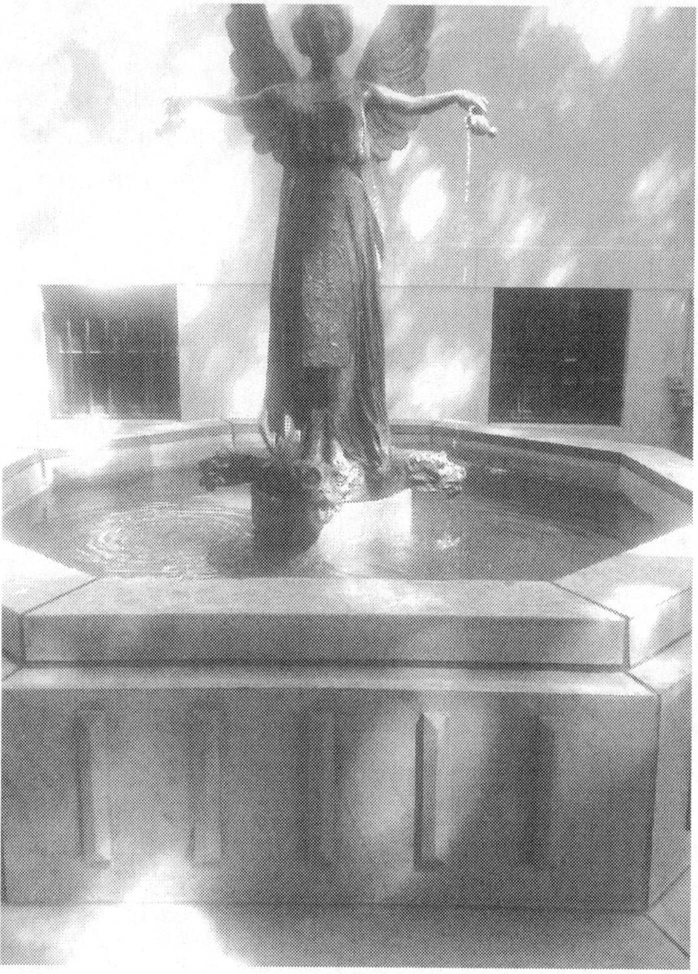

Chapter Nineteen

Open Your Eye's And Wake Up

Let us wake up and see how God's plan for the world and for our lives is unfolding before our very eyes. Our life is in his hands. Open your eyes and realize how God has freed you from so many things that had you bound, and gave you a better mind.

To see how to live a better life read Ephesians 5:14-20, *"Wherefore he saith, Awake thou that sleepest, and arise from the dead, and Christ shall give thee light. See then that ye walk circumspectly, not as fools, but as wise, redeeming the time, because the days are evil. Wherefore be ye not unwise, but understanding what the will of the Lord is. And be not drunk with wine, wherein is excess; but be filled with the Spirit; speaking to yourselves in psalms and hymns and spiritual songs, singing and making melody in your heart to the Lord; giving thanks always for all things unto God and the Father in the name of our Lord Jesus Christ."*

Let us open our eyes and wake up and walk upright, living peacefully.

Wake up people of the world. Because we were sleep walking in the dark, we allowed Satan to steal years on top of years out of our lives.

Wake up and let him that stole, steal no more.

Nothing comes to a sleeper but a dream and a nightmare; arise and fulfill God's plan for your life, recognize the gift in you and who died for you.

Many people in the world and those of God have closed their eyes and fallen asleep in the middle of the day; open your eyes and wake up! We have too many people sleeping and dreaming. Stop dreaming and face reality!

1 Thessalonians 5:5 reads "Ye are all the children of light, and the children of the day: we are not of the night, nor of darkness."

Verse 6 reads **"Therefore let us not sleep as do others; but let us watch and be sober."**

Let us wake up with a sober mind and a controlling attitude.

Verse 7 says, **"For they that sleep, sleep in the night, and they that be drunken are drunken in the night."**

Verse 8 reads, **"But let us, who are of the day, be sober, putting on the breastplate of faith and love; and for an helmet, the hope of salvation."**

Verse 9 reads, **"For God hath not appointed us to wrath, but to obtain salvation by our Lord Jesus Christ."**

Verse 10 reads, **"Who died for us, that, whether we wake or sleep, we should live together with him."**

The God I serve is able to open up blinded eyes. He wakes you up when you've been sleeping.

God touch you with his finger of love. God is a keeper, He will keep you on your toes, and your body from been frozen if you know what I mean.

After we wake up, let us clean up our minds and hearts, which are dirty and need to be cleaned. Thank God for Jesus, who looked beyond our faults and saw our needs.

Our God is a good God. He's been better to us than we've been to ourselves. He will give you a good mind after waking up with a bad mind; He will take away the bad and dirty thoughts and replace them with good and righteous thoughts.

The God I serve will give you a brand new start and a clean heart. He will take out the dirty walls of filth and hatred and rebuild new walls clean and spotless, filled with a new love from God above.

People of the world today have made a mess of their lives and need to work on cleaning up the mess they have made by allowing God in their lives to help them clean up what they've messed up.

Let God come into your heart and clean house. He will wipe the slate clean.

The blood of Jesus will wash away all the guilty stain of sin that need to be washed clean.

James 4:7-8 reads, *"Submit yourselves therefore to God, resist the devil and he flee from you."*

Put up a fight and fight that devil back when he comes to beat you down.

James 4:8 says, ***"Draw nigh to God and He will draw nigh to you. Cleanse your hands ye sinner and purify your hearts ye double-minded."***

Let us get made up minds to serve the one and only true God almighty. Let us begin to clean up old bad debts, and old bad habits and nasty ways.

Let us clean up our speech of filthy evil communication.

May you listen to these words of wisdom and take heed to this teaching. May God bless you and forever keep you.

You're Messenger Jimmy J.

Chapter Twenty

God Opened My Eyes and Let Me See I Was Naked

Thank God for the clothes He gives us to wear both physically and spiritually. Thank Him for showing us that He cares. Many of us are in need of a new wardrobe many of our clothes have been worn-out and torn, rip and stripped.

The devil has been warring in our minds and wearing us down, tearing us down for far too long. Ripping us off with this and stripping us out of that, stealing our joy, taking whatever he can leaving us naked and unprotected.

Take a look at yourself and see if you have any holes in your clothes.

Those of us who are supposed to be fully clothed dressed in love, take a look at yourself and you will see many holes in your Christian love walk! Take a look at yourself and you will see that you're only partially displaying the love God expects of us to display each and every day.

Take a look at yourself and see the holes in your clothes of commitment and loyalty towards God. Be clothed in love. Dress yourselves spiritually, shining bright, armed with the sword of God's word. Walk upright and be ready to fight. Take a look at yourself and you see the holes in your clothes, the lack of respect for God. Take a look at yourself and see holes instead of honor for God.

Take a look at yourself and see the holes in your clothes of humility.

May you become more humble and less arrogant and disrespectable to God.

1Peter 1:6-7 reads, ***"Humble yourselves therefore under the mighty hand of God, that he may He exalt you in due time casting all your cares upon him for he cares for you."***

Take a look at yourselves and the holes in your clothes, let God clothed you. Let God repair you if you're broken, He'll fix you up and clean you up when you're dirty, and He'll pick up when you're down.

He will straighten you up and dress you up when your life is all messed up. He will straighten it out, He will He'll help you get in line with His word so you may line up with His word so that we may become more closer to measuring up to His word.

And be clothed so you will not be found naked. Dress yourselves in the amour of God, put on the breastplate of righteousness and walk up right. Put your trust in God and depend on Him.

When you're falling over here and falling over there, losing your grip, keep your hand in the Master's hand.

When your feet begins to slip, causing you to detour from God's plans, this is when we need to call on the Lord and lean on His guidance and let Him prop you up when you're falling down.

The Lord will be our leaning post and a fence of protection all around us.

If we ever needed the Lord, we sure do need him now because were living in some bad times. War, hurricanes, and tornados, sweep through towns destroying houses and land, taking the lives of many.

We're livings in hard times of poverty; people are robbing, stealing, and killing one another.

Now is the time to be clothed and walk in the footsteps of Jesus. If you're walking in the footsteps of Jesus and your life doesn't line up with His teaching, then you need to seek the Lord for direction, and line up with His word!

If you're staggering in this Christian walk, and off balance, causing your mind to waiver and wonder, God is able to help you become stable, rooted and grounded, suited and booted, ready for war, fighting on the front line, being attacked on every side, getting hit from all angles.

Sometimes we get hit so hard by the enemy, Satan, it knocks us off track, leaving us dazed, causing us to lose our focus and be off balance.

Thank God for Jesus, who received you, stabilized you, to help you win this fight. We are a direct target for the enemy of Satan, who targets us, aiming to kill us, using evil and wicked thoughts to mislead us down the road of destruction. He uses heavy artillery, firing repeatedly and shooting us down daily, but I want to let it be known that we are not alone. We have many troops and soldiers on the battle field, fighting with us and for us. We have the sergeant of arms of the Holy Ghost who will teach you.

He will lead and guide you, to show you which way to go to keep you from getting lost, smoked or toasted on the battle field. We also have the chief commander, King Jesus, who commands us and tells us how we must fight our enemy Satan. This commander-in-charge also said if I am with you, who can be against you?

He also said; *cast all your cares on me.* Just be still and I'll fight your battles! Prepare yourselves for battle, even though King Jesus said he will fight our battles for us.

We still must arm ourselves with the shield of faith, and the sword of God's word. Put on the helmet of salvation and the breastplate of righteousness and shod your feet with the preparation of the gospel of peace.

Feet shod with the gospel of peace means we must run on and spread the *good news!* It means we must run in this war and fight, it means we must stand for the righteousness of Jesus Christ. Let us be clothed and prepared to run in this race that has been set before us.

Let us be a helper, one to another, striving to make it into the Kingdom of Heaven. Jesus spoke a word to us in Matthew 25:35-40 saying, *"For I was hungry and you gave Me food; I was thirsty and you gave Me drink; I was a stranger and you took Me in; I was naked and you clothed Me; I was sick and you visited Me; I was in prison and you came to Me.'*

"Then the righteous will answer Him, saying, "Lord, when did we see You hungry and feed You, or thirsty and give You drink? When did we see You a stranger and take You in or naked and clothe You? Or when did we see You sick, or in prison, and come to You?' And the King will answer and say to them, 'Assuredly, I say to you, inasmuch as you did it to one of the least of these My brethren, you did it to Me."

Open your eyes and see all the nakedness around you and begin to clothe yourselves and others.

Matthew 6:24-25 reads, *"No man can serve two masters; for either he will hate the one, and love the other ye cannot serve God and mammon.*

Therefore I say unto take no thought for your life what ye should eat or what ye shall drink nor for your body, what you should put on. Is not life more than meat and the body more than raiment?"

Do not let Satan make you take off the uniform God has given you. Keep on your war clothes; do not let the enemy of Satan find you naked, and unprotected.

Matt 6:26-30 reads, *"Look at the birds of the air, for they neither sow nor reap nor gather into barns; yet your heavenly Father feeds them. Are you not of more value than they? Which of you by worrying can add one cubit to his stature?*

"So why do you worry about clothing? Consider the lilies of the field, how they grow: they neither toil nor spin; and yet I say to you that even Solomon in all his glory was not arrayed like one of these. Now if God so clothes the grass of the field, which today is, and tomorrow is thrown into the oven, will He not much more clothe you, O you of little faith?"

Let God dress you and clothe your minds with peace that passed all understanding. Let God dress you up on the inside and clean you up and give you a clean heart dressed in love, from God above. If God take care of the Lillie of the field surely he will take of those who are his and those who do his will.

Verse 31, *"Therefore take no thought saying what shall we eat or what shall we drink/or withal shall be clothed."*

Jesus is speaking to us and telling us, do not be worried. I have already figured out your needs and I know what you stand in need of. I will bless you with the things you stand in need of and give you the desires of your hearts.

God is saying trust in me and I will provide for you.

"His eyes where as a flame of fire, on his head where many crowns; and he had a name written that no man

knew but himself. He was clothed with vesture dipped in blood and His name is called the word God."

The clothes that Jesus was wearing were a possession of pureness. This man was hung high and died for you and me. His clothes were soaked in blood.

He made an investment, paid with his life. He bought back a world that was lost in sin. He clothed the world, covered them with his blood and washed them clean.

Let God wash you clean dress you in love. Be fully clothed if you're naked. Many of us are half dressed and some of us are naked.

I hope something I said will help you dress better, look better, do better, and feel better. That's the end of this message. God opened my eyes and let me see that I was naked.

You're Messenger Jimmy J.

Chapter Twenty-One

The Good and the Bad

There have been many times bad things happen to good people, things that the devil meant for bad, but God turn things around into good and made good things happen in your life.

Do good and good will follow you, do bad and you will reap what you sow. Sad to say, but bad things will find their way back in your life and come back to hurt you.

We have to take the good with the bad, the bitter with the sweet, and feast on the meat of God's Word; that will carry us through the good times and the bad times. Amen.

Praise the Lord Saints! Thank Him for the good times as well as the bad.

Thank Him when you're happy and thank Him when you are sad.

All of our good days out weigh our bad days, those have been times and days well spent. When we wake up feeling good like a child of God should, walking around in the blessings of God. Happy and striving to walk up right, doing things that please God.

There have also been times when we wake up with a bad mind (thinking devilish thoughts) doing bad things, but either way it was God that woke us up.

God's Spoken Word In Plain View

I believe that it is safe to say all of our good days out weigh our bad days some days may be better than others, everyday is a good day, because we could be six feet underground, sleeping in our grave smothered with dirt; but thanks be to God we are alive and well. We are still able to move around and breathe God's air; we can touch, see, taste, feel, smell, and hear.

May you listen and hear God's Word, and not let it just come in one ear and out the other ear.

Instead take heed to what is being said from all the different speakers of God's Word. Grab hold of something in God's Word that has been spoken, and it will help you if you let it soak in.

God is good, He might not come when you want Him too, but he's always right on time. There have been times when God lets us go through the day with a peace of mind, and love in our hearts toward all mankind.

He also has put a smile on your face, so let us be thankful, and thank God for the warmth of His love, unlike the cold blooded so called love that comes from the world that is supposed to be good, but will give you many bad experiences. Once you experience the Love of God, His love will keep you and protect you at all times, so let us be thankful for things being as well as they are.

Thank God for the sunshine in the day that makes us all feel good even when we are feeling bad.

Praise the Lord! We all know every day is not going to be sunny; some days are going to be filled with rain, that's the way some will feel from day to day. Some days we will be filled with joy and then there will be days when those joyful smiles will be turned into frowns because of the bad times and burdens in our mind.

Let us remember trouble doesn't always last, sometimes we may go through some hard and difficult times, suffering with both physical and emotional pain. Some people's pain can hurt so bad that it drives them insane; thank God we're not suffering pain to that degree.

We should be thankful and grateful, recognizing how God has raised us up above the flood of high waters.

God has lifted us up above many difficult and dangerous situations. May those of you who have not yet came to the realization of what God is doing in the lives of His people, soon come to the realization of God's rescuing power and realize the good in God and the power that will carry you through those bad, painful, suicidal, situations that many of us have experienced, but did not know we were killing ourselves slowly and deliberately, destroying our minds.

Satan flooded our minds with these bad thoughts to become doers of evil and wrong things.

Many of us today who know how to be bad and do wrong, we did wrong. Many of us today have experienced and tasted the bad life of evil and doing wrong, we also have had some days when we ourselves displayed bad behavior.

Many of us today are still displaying bad behaviors. Many of our minds are still entangled in the affairs of this world, but God has raised us up above the floods and fiery waters of Satan, and the deep pitfalls that cause one to stay down.

God has lifted us up, we do not have to continue to swim in sin, and we can float through life hanging on God's Word by striving to live right

As we pass thorough the mean and evil streets where evil is done and people enjoy living wrong; let us remember God is still on the throne.

God is able to turn our bad days into good days. All of our good days out weigh our bad days

God is a good God, that's why he sent His son Jesus to die for our sins. Thank you for sending your son Jesus into the world to die so that we might live.

Back in the Bible days, the world was swimming in sin. It had so much sin that the Lord thy God regretted that He had made man, and He wouldn't stand for any more of the world's sins, so He destroyed the world.

God sent his son Jesus to die for all the sins of the world.

John 3:16 states, *"For God so loved the world He gave His only begotten son that whosoever believeth in Him should not perish, but have everlasting life."*

Praise the Lord Saints! When Jesus came into the world He brought life, love and peace. He intended for us to live the good life.

Spread His love and be at peace today.

Everyone may not grab a hold of this, or put it in their hearts and minds to help themselves stand firm in these hard and difficult times in this unfair world of unbelievers of God's Word.

This makes us appear unfruitful in the deliverance of God's Word to the unbelievers who look upon you.

Be **doers** of God's Word and not just **hearers** only.

God is able to do all things! He will help you become who you ought to be in Christ and live right because He already know we're not living like we should be in Christ.

God sent his son Jesus to be our healer and deliverer; He healed the sick and made them well, and let them continue to dwell in the land of the living

From one touch of his healing hands, Jesus is willing and able to deliver you from anything that may have you bound. He's able to deliver you from any situation that may hold you down. God is able to turn any situation around; Jesus is a heart fixer and a mind regulator.

I know this personally, because He fixed it for me. He gave me a clean heart and renewed my mind. Things I used to do, I don't desire to do those things any more, places I used to go, I don't go there anymore.

The Word of God and the Spirit of Jesus will clean you up from being dirty and dusty, or rusty like an old penny to being clean and shining like a new dime.

Jesus will turn the old you into the new and improved you; one who is now living a life committed to do God's will, unlike the old you. There are many of us who once lived a life of crime.

Thank God for giving us a new mind, so we can do better in life, and strive to live the good life, God is able to turn our bad days into good days.

If you think back from last year to this year, your good days will outweigh your bad days.

If you think back from last month to this month, your good days will outweigh your bad days.

Every day is a good day. Sometimes we experience bad times and hardships throughout the course of a day, but I must say, it's still good to be in the land of the living instead of being dead and dying in a world of sin.

As long as we are alive and well we can do many things.

There is one thing we can do for sure through good times or bad times, we can always come to Christ Jesus and ask Him to forgive us of your sins. Repentance of your sins means to be Godly sorry for the wrongs that you have done to hurt other people as well as yourself.

God will forgive you, and welcome you into His kingdom with open arms.

He will grab hold of you, and take you to a higher level of life, a better place. He'll take away your sins and begin a new *relationship* with you.

He'll take away your fears and dry your tears. He will take away all of your worries, because He said in his Word cast all of your cares on Him because He will care for you. While we are worrying about different situations in life that have become burdens to us; He has already figured it out!

God already has solved the problem.

You're Messenger Jimmy J

CIRCLE OF LIGHT
CHURCH
REV. JEFF JOHNSON JR. PASTOR
FOUNDED 1997
WELCOM

Chapter Twenty-Two

Good Hearted People with Bad Minds

Thank Him when you're up, and thank Him when you're down.

Many of us have good intentions, a good heart. Many times we have intentions on doing the right thing and end up doing things that are wrong and displeasing to God, because many of us have a good heart, but a bad mind.

Many hearts that were made to give life and show love have been made to welcome in Satan, who has caused many hearts to show hatred and become separated from God the Father. In the process of staying connected to the father of lies, the *vine* of hatred is growing throughout the states. Wrapping around our hearts, sparring none, choking out love, peace and killing many people for fun!

Some of our hearts are glad and some of our hearts are sad, many hearts are mad and unsatisfied, filled with lies. God gave us all a true heart, pure and clean, but man defiled his own heart with *wicked* things.

God looks at the heart of man and sees all the dirt and filth within our hearts.

God still loves us all, and wants us to call on Him when we get into trouble and need His help. He said in His word, *He would never leave us nor forsake us.*

His love never departed from us. God is a good God, because the more we do wrong and the dirtier our hearts and minds become, the more He opens his arms and welcome us into his heavenly home.

The heart of God beats in all of us, remember He sent His son Jesus to die for us so that we might live.

God lives in us and in our hearts, that's where He is.

Many of us have a good heart and a bad mind. When God gave us this heart of love it was once purified, but now when He looks on the hearts of today's men and women, boys and girls, He probably gets angry at the world and wonder why people would rather live dirty and filthy lives, instead of being clean and spotless. How do people live with so much dirt and filth clogging up their hearts then he will say only by my grace and mercy realizing a good sterilization is needed to clean these hearts of men women boys and girl of today's world.

May we open up our hearts to God and give it to Jesus so he can wash them clean you only get one heart take care of it and keep it clean and be careful of what you put in it.

Eat of his word taste and see how good it is, and it will bring goodness into your life and help you walk upright in the fullness of Christ.

Jesus spoke a word and said men praise me with their mouth but their hearts is far from me."

Roman 10:10 reads, "for with the heart man believeth unto righteousness and with the mouth confession is made unto salvation."

If you believe in your hearts and conceive righteous thoughts on the daily basic you can achieve your rightful place in heaven."

Matt. 15:19 says, *"For out of the heart proceed evil thoughts murder, adulteries, fornication, thefts, false witness, and blasphemies."*

These are the things that defile a man; but to eat with unwashed hands do not defile a man.

Let us not defile our self with all these different things of the world, and trouble your hearts and worry your minds.

John 14:1 says, *"Let not your heart be trouble; ye believe in God believe also in me."*

James 4:8 says, *"Draw nigh to God and he will draw nigh to you.*

Cleanse your hands ye sinners and purified hearts ye double minded."

Stop playing with Satan so you can keep your hands clean

Because he do not play fare, and he do not care about you are hurting you. Playtime is over time out for playing around with the devil and his followers,

It's time to stay focus and study to show ourselves approve unto God.

We all have some work to do on ourselves let us take a look at our wrong and study on correcting our wrongs into rights.

God is able to give you a good mind even after waking up with a bad mind; bad thoughts will flow through our minds throughout the day.

We hath to pray and ask God for forgiveness and ask him to give us a better mind, many of times we hath to cast down bad imagination because many of times bad and negative thoughts will flow into our minds we might find ourselves acting on those bad thoughts.

That the time when we need to call on Jesus for whatever the reason may be, and say look lord I know I been wrong, and I know you know what I'm going through I need you to come rescue me get this devil off of me.

And he will come see about you, God is able he's able to pick up a bow down head.

He able to turn your bad days into good days. He able to give you peace in the mist of confusion

He able to give you all a good mind even after waking up with a bad mind, he able to turn your frowns into smile.

God is able to turn your sorrows into Joy God is able to do the unthinkable and save you from sinking deeper into the region of a bad mind, causing you to fall further behind.

He able to let you know I'm God almighty, he's able to let you know do not play with me because I'm no play toy, many of us are playing in the field and reluctant to do his will but is willing to do fulfill the desires of him who come to give you a bad mind.

Many of us are playing with bad thoughts failing to seek after the lord and walk in righteousness and think on good and righteous thoughts.

Jeopardizing the most important a vital parts of the body which is your hearts and minds, many of us are playing with their own hearts and minds.

Many of us are playing with the church many of us in the body of the church, are playing in the field getting our hands dirty because we touch and taste the things that are forbidden of God.

Many of our hands are dirty because were still being flirty with temptation temping to pick up the fruits of evil

But God is calling out in the field saying its time out playing on the devil turf. Come on home my son my daughter my child my lost love ones with good hearts and bad minds.

Many people of this world we live in are lost and hurting trying to find they way back home

Searching for rest and peace, give foolishness a rest come home and rest with me God your Father and my son Jesus. Come on home and wash your dirty hands, come on home and wash the filth out of your minds, come on home and wash and cleanse your hearts, come on home and take a bath in the blood of Jesus.

Come sit at the table with me and eat of the things I have prepared for you.

Psalm 23:5 reads, *"Thou prepares a table before me in the presence of mine enemies: thou anointed my head with oil; my cup runneth over."*

Verse 23:6 *"Surely goodness and mercy shall follow me all the days of my life; and I will dwell in the house of the lord for ever Amen."*

There's many of good hearted people with bad minds and dirty hands who been giving a new heart and renewed mind, and clean hands.

Matt. 6:21 *"Tells us for where your treasures are there will your heart be also."*

May we treasure the things of God so our hearts will be found in the treasure of his love treasure this word which is written for you put in your hearts and feed off it daily until you get full of God's spirit?

Treasure yourself because you are worthy, you been bought with a price and your worth more than gold and your hearts shall abide under the shadow of the most high God almighty.

We been bought, and the price he paid for us is greater than any amount of money anyone can ever pay, he purchase us with his blood, God is a heart fixer's and a mind regulator if your heart is broken and your hurting, let God fix's your hearts and sooth the pain, if your mind is confused and your mind is bad causing you to do bad things and behave badly, give it to Jesus

And he will regulate that confuse mind and help you to think right.

If you have a bad mind talk to Jesus and tell him to give you better mind if

Your hands are dirty put your hands in the masters hands and they will become clean instantly, and you will know for yourself you been wash and the dirt been removed.

Lift those dirty hands in the air, and reach out to God let him shower you with his love from above, good hearted people with bad minds may you let

God bless you and strengthen your hearts renew your minds and cleanse

Your dirty hands.

2Cor. 6:17 tells us, *"Wherefore come out from among them, and be separated, saith the lord and touch not the unclean thing; and I will receive you unto myself."*

Verse 18 says, *"And I will be a father unto you and ye shall be my sons and daughters, saith the Lord almighty."*

May God bless you!

You're Messenger Jimmy J.

Chapter Twenty-Three

Let go of the bad things in your Past

&

Chapter Twenty-Four

Grab A Hold Of The Good Things In Your Present Life

Praise the Lord, and thank Him for things being as well as they are.

Keep reaching out for God; He's not that far away, He's right here in the deep part of our hearts. Amen.

Cor. 5:17 reads *"Therefore if any man is in Christ he is a new creature; old things are passed away; behold, all thing are become new."*

Once you come in connection with Jesus walking in a new direction.

And begins to walk with the Lord you will become closer and closer to the Lord Jesus.

And if for any reason you shall fall God will send His angels to come and see about His child or Jesus Himself will come and pick you up; if any man be in Christ he should walk with his head up.

Keeping his eyes on the prize and his mind on God and walk where he lead you and follow the footsteps of Jesus and He will lead us closer to the door where He stands with arms stretched wide to welcome us inside of Heaven.

If any man be in Christ He is given a new mind that gives you a new mindset that is willing to be obedient and taught.

He gives you a new mind to think good and righteous thoughts.

If any man be in Christ He is also given a new heart with new love, compassion and concerns of other.

If any man be in Christ he is not the same, because the old man died and the new man live; May this new man that lives in you be used and live a life unto God.

May this new man walk according to the teaching he been taught.

Let love abide in you as you walk where Jesus guides you.

Walk in love and not hate, Endure hardships and hang on in there my friend; Run on and see what's the end going to be like and continue to stand for Righteousness.

If any man be in Christ he must suffer like Christ and he shall also reign with Christ and be given strength and might, and made to shine like bright lights in darkness.

In Jesus there is no darkness, and if we are new creatures in Christ, then the darkness in us must flee; Let Jesus wash those dark spots clean in our lives.

If any man be in Christ he is given a new way of talking, he don't talk the same that new man in Christ will be trying to introduce someone else to Christ, that new man who use to have a filthy mouth now speak with clean meaningful and wholesome words of encouragement and love.

Being in Christ is where we need to be bowing at His feet doing a new thing letting Christ rule supreme striving to go higher to get a closer walk with Him.

Old things are passed away; behold all things are become new. Meaning we're going to hath to let go some of these old negative things that we are holding on to that got a grip on us keeping us tied to that old man who died. Break loose and let the new man lives to do God's will and walk in a newness.

Meaning we need to be done with some of those old things that are not of God let us not pass the old bad things we done down to generation to generation.

Let us live a new life and do new things. Many of us are still feeding the old man; the food we're feeding him should be given to the new man.

Many of us are still listening to the old man letting him lead us to a place where God done brought us from.

Many of us are still being obedient to the old man and doing the things he tell us being disobedient to the new man who tells you to do the right thing and lead you down the path of righteousness.

Many of us who are suppose to be new creatures in Christ is still walking in the old sinful man who suppose to be dead.

Giving opportunities to that old man to come back alive in our lives so we must die daily and die to self and the old thought and behavior which hasn't gotten us nowhere we can say we're really proud of so.

Let us try something new, and try Jesus put your belief and trust in him and soon you'll be able to say I'm proud of the move I made and I'm glad I tried to do things a new way.

Keep trying until you succeed don't give in and I pray give that devil an upper cup hitter down below. Then stand up and face him toe to toe and let him know I'm not running any more I got King Jesus on my side.

And I'm standing up and fighting for mines, then watch that lying devil flee and run out the door and the victory will be yours.

2 Cor. 5:18 says, **"And all things are of God, who hath Reconciled us to himself by Jesus Christ, and hath given to us the Ministry of Reconciliation."**

Everything we do is done in his strength, his grace, his Mercy, and his love.

We all been reconciled and brought back to God by Jesus. It was Jesus that paid the cost to save this lost and dying world, it was Jesus that picked up a bow down head, and regulated a confused mind.

It was Jesus that lifted our spirited when we were heavy laden and burden down.

It was Jesus that gave us all a better mind time and time again, and brought us all back from being lost in a world of sin, it was Jesus that brought us over the bridge of trouble waters, it was Jesus that brought us into the land of safety and place our feet on solid grounds.

It was Jesus that brought us life, it was Jesus that brought us love, it was Jesus that brought us a mighty long way, and it is Jesus who's still bringing us today.

He brought wisdom and knowledge; he brought each one of us safely throughout the year and kept us here, Thank God for Jesus and for bringing back all those who were lost, many of us lost our way in life.

But Jesus found us and gave us directions many of us lost track of time and have fail to prevail and move forward in life and has fail behind, many of us has lost our mind, being caught up, bind up, and wind up like a puppet on string, singing Satan song and doing wrong; falling into the traps he laid to hinder you and hold you down to keep you from rising up and saving some other lost soul Satan knows what buttons to push to make you move.

He even knows what button to push to make you lose control.

He knows what button to push to make you sing and dance to his beat He has study all of us and learn different ways how to steal, kill and destroy us.

Jesus comes to give us life so we may live, he comes to save us and protect us from the destroyer.

Jesus comes to give peace and set us free from sin.

He come to help us save ourselves so we can help save and tell somebody else, who brought us over, and how we made it over.

Somebody need to tell the world Jesus is real somebody tell the world Jesus has come and gone and left his blood stain on Calvary he left his blood stain of love in our hearts, he left his blood stain of peace in our minds and he died bravely for all mankind.

He gave us the ministry of reconciliation so we can minister to someone else and help bring back lost soul to Christ.

He gave us the ministry of reconciliation to tell of his goodness.

His power, his might, his strength, his love, tell somebody how God brought you over, tell somebody how you know God is able to calm the storm in thy life tell somebody your testimony and how God fixed it for you, tell somebody God is good, and what he did for me he'll do the same thing for you.

Roman 2:11 "for there is no respect of person with God."

What he does for one person he does the same for another person.

He died once for all so that all may live to do his will.

That the end of this message let go bad things in your past life, and grab hold to the good things. May God bless you!

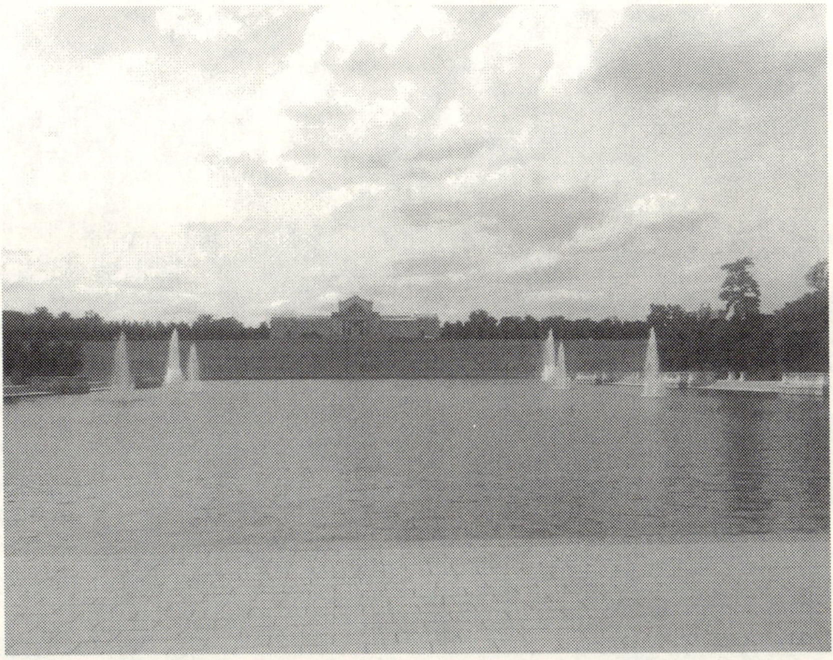

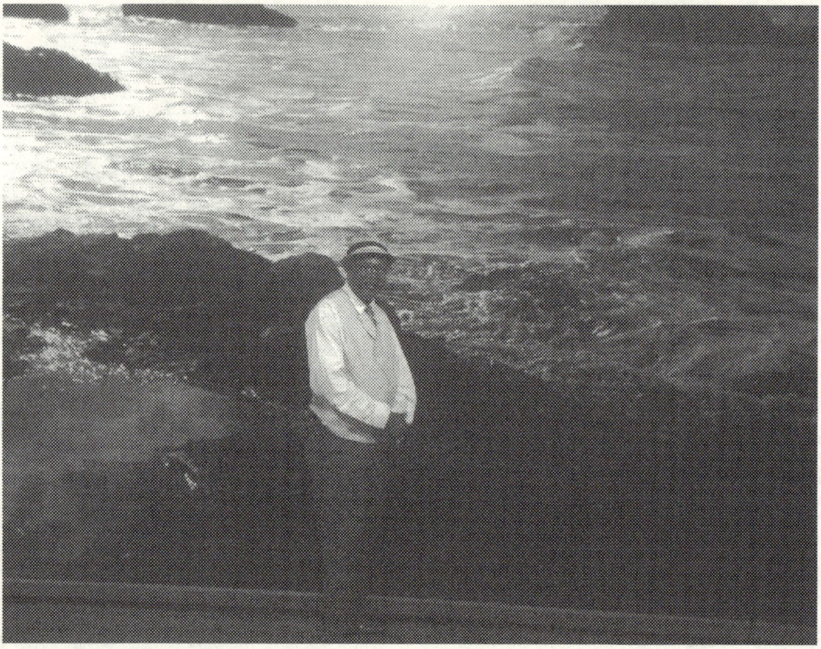

Chapter Twenty-Five

Trust and Obey

Praise the Lord, and give thanks unto God.

Psalm 37:3 *"Trust in the lord and do good so shalt thou dwell in the land and verily thou shalt be fed."*

To trust is to put confidence in someone or something, and believe in that thing or someone; so if we say we trust in God then we should obey meaning to follow his commands or guidance.

John 14:21-26 reads *"He that hath my commandment, and keepeth them. He it is that loveth me, and he that loveth me: shall be loved of my father, and I will love him and manifest myself to him."*

Verse 22 Judas saith unto him, Not Is-car'-iot, *"Lord, how is it that thou wilt manifest thyself unto us, and not unto the world?"*

Verse 23 reads, Jesus answered and said unto him, *"If a man loves me he will keep my words; and my Father will love him and we will come unto him and make our abode with him."*

Verse 24 *"He that love me not keepeth not my sayings; and the words which ye hear is not mine, but the Father which sent me."*

Verse 25 *"These things have I spoken unto you being yet present with you."*

Verse 26 *"But the comforter which is the holy Ghost, whom the father will send in my name, he shall teach you all things and bring all things to your remembrance whatsoever I have said to you."*

So when we trust God then we should obey his word, then we should let his word be our guidance if we do that then were making great success in our

Christian walk, if were already doing that then were being obedient to God word.

Now obedient is the key the most important decision we can make is to be obedient to God word.

Obedient leads to deliverance disobedient leads to destruction.

Psalm 33:18-21, tells us *"Behold the eyes of the lord is up on them who fear him, upon them that hope in his mercy; to deliver their souls from death, and keep them alive in famine."*

Verse 20 says, *"Our souls waiteth for the lord; he is our help and our shield."*

Verse 21 says, *"For our hearts shall rejoice in him, because we have trusted in his holy name."*

Trust and obey do not hesitate, trust him he said in his word he will never leave you nor forsake you, give your mind over to God and trust him at the drop of a dime.

And do not delay to obey God spoken word, and strive to live right and do right and never lose sight of Jesus because he's the reason why we live.

I had to trust him many of times in my life, and if he had not come to my rescue to save me, protected me.

And come by to see about me when he did it wouldn't be no me, it's because of him that I live.

And I recommend Jesus to anyone because I trust him and he is real he came to my rescue many of times. I know him for myself, trust me when I tell you

H e's a mind regulator reason I know because he regulated my mind many of times he gave me a good mind when all I had was a bad mind.

I thank him for giving me a better mind, trust me when I say God will pick you up when your down.

I been down, I lost all I had at one time, everything I own was gone even part of my mind, I was lost.

But he help me find myself trust me when I say he's a heart fixer, I been broken, my spirit been wounded I been made to feel low I been down,

I walked in poverty, I been shot in the head left for dead, I been down, I laid

On my sick bed with no guarantees on getting back up.

I had to call on Jesus and trust him.

Palms 34:17-22 reads *"**The righteous cry, and the lord heareth and delivereth them out of their troubles.***

The lord is nigh unto them that are of a broken heart and saveth such that

Be of a contrite spirit; if you have sorrow in your hearts trust in the lord andhewill bring you joy.

Many are the affliction of the righteous but the lord delivereth them out of them all.

Evil shall slay the wicked; and they that hate righteous shall be desolate; let us not hate the righteous, instead love them and admire them for been Christ like."

Jesus stood for righteous and was admire by many, in the same manner many of us should admire other who stand for righteous whom trying to be Christ-like.

Trust and obey the lord redeemeth the soul of his servants and none of them that trust in him shall be desolate.

Titus 2:7-9 reads *"**In all things shewing incorruptness** meaning that your showing goodness many of us today display just opposite instead of showing goodness many of us have a pattern of showing bad behavior and nasty ways.*

Which gives us a corrupt spirit within, but when you do good and have God spirit in you it shows outwardly."

Titus 2:9 tells us to *"**Exhort servants to be obedient unto their masters, and please them well in all things not answering again."***

God's Spoken Word In Plain View

Trust in lord and obey his word, obedient brings deliverance, deliverance brings victory, meaning you have won the battle over that which came to bring you down or destroy you.

John 10:10 tells us that the thief cometh not but to steal, kill, and destroy: [Thief] meaning the devil.

But Jesus comes that they might have life; we should be quick to take heed to the word of the God.

Titus 2:10 says *"Not purlonging, but showing all good fedelty; that they may adorn the doctrine of God our savior in All things, meaning to be loyal, faithful, the salvation of the lord hath appeared to all men, meaning he came to free us from our sins."*

Ask God to come into your hearts and repent and turn from your own ways and turn to him and be saved.

Let God save you from the penalty of sin which is death, Jesus Christ came and died for our sin, and then rose again so we can live, when Jesus brought salvation unto all men he saved us from destruction.

John 3:16 *"For God so love the world that he gave his only be gotten son, that whosoever believeth in him should not perish but have everlasting life."*

Verse 17 *"For God sent not his son into the world to condemned the world ; but that the world through him might be saved."*

Giving thanks unto the father which has made us meet to be part taker of the inheritance of the saint; in the light who has translated us into the kingdom of his dear son; in whom we have redemption through his blood, even for the forgiveness of your sins.

The word meet means he has qualified you, qualifying you in such a way that you will be strengthen with all power according to his glories might so you might have great endurance and patience to share in the inheritance of the saints in the kingdom of light, Trust and obey.

Just like Moses trusted in the lord and obeys his commands, it was by God and through Moses obedience. Israel was delivered out of Egypt.

The land of slavery Moses said unto his people, remember this day in which ye came out of the house of bondage; for by the strength of the lord.

God is good not did he only bring the children of Israel out of Egypt he stayed with them and protected them, by showing them which way to go.

Exodus 13:21 tell us *"The lord went before them by day in a pillar of a cloud to lead the way, and by night a pillar of fire to give them light, to go by day and night. He took not away the pillar of cloud by day nor did he take away the pillar of fire by night."*

Thank be to God who looks after us day and night protects us and keeps us safe.

Many of us today is still in bondage and need to be deliver from many different area's in our life.

God's Spoken Word In Plain View

Obedient to God word can bring deliverance to whomever trust and obey his word.

There once where three men over the affairs of the province of Babylon; whose name were meshach, shadrach and Abednego who trusted in God, and would not bow down and worship golden images nor worship any God except their own.

These men were cast into the burning fiery furnace because they were disobedient to the king's wishes. Just like us who are disobedient to God, we finds ourselves going through the fire.

Now in expect of their disobedient to the kings wishes they did right so they may stay obedient to the wishes of God.

Were not to put our trust in man, because man cannot save us but God can, and because they trusted in God he sent his angel and delivered his servants that trusted in him.

Let us trust and obey God's word disobedient brings destruction, to disobey open up room to obey the devil whom will lead you to destruction, and many there be that which go in there at; because straight is the gate and narrow is the way which leads unto life, and few there be that find it.

Obedient not only leads you to deliverance but also unto life.

You cannot be disobedient to God word and make through the straight gate.

If you be disobedient to God word, it's a good chance you will be going through the wide gate, and broad is the way, meaning there will be many on their way to destruction.

If you want to see life and have life more abundantly, trust in the lord and obey his word.

Psalm 25:2 reads, **"O my God I trust in thee let me not be a shamed, let not my enemies triumph over me."**

Psalm 27:1 says, *"The lord is my light and my salvation; whom shall I fear the lord is the strength of my life of whom shall I be afraid?"*

As long as we have God on our side, protecting us, we do not hath to be afraid of no one may you put your trust in God and obey May God bless you and keep you.

Your Messenger Jimmy J.

Chapter Twenty-Six

Believing and Succeeding

Praise the Lord!

To believe is to have faith or confidence in someone or something, to accept as being true.

If you believe Christ is the son of God, the one who fed five thousand people with five loaves of bread two fishes, the one who healed the sick, and turn water into wine, the one who gave sight to the blind, he's the one who gave us life yet while we were dying.

Who also gave his own life to pay for the penalty of our sin? Now if you believe Jesus died for you, me, and the entire world then you should also believe he rose again and now sits at the right hand of the father.

Now if you believe all that to be true then you should be succeeding to achieve that which ye believe in; succeeding is to be successful. So if we are believing and succeeding, then we should be following what we believe in. if we believe in Jesus Christ then we should obey his teaching.

If were following his teaching then and only then is when your going to succeed to achieve that in which you believe in?

Continue to follow his teaching, to achieve means to bring about accomplishment to be successful Ask yourself what have I accomplish,

So if we are achieving that which we believe in then our walk with Jesus will be successful John3:16, *"For God so loved the world that he gave his only begotten son, that whosoever believeth in him should not perish, but have everlasting life."*

Verse 17 *"For God sent not his son into the world to condemn the world; but through him the world might be saved."*

He that believeth on him is not condemned; but he that believeth not is already condemned already because he has not believed in the name of the only begotten son of God.

John 5: 24 reads, *"Verily, verily, I say unto you he that sent me hath everlasting life, and shall not come into condemnation, but has passed from death to life."*

John 6:35 reads, *"And Jesus said I am the bread of life and also the son of God he that cometh to me shall never hunger and he that believeth on me shall never thirst."*

St. John 1:1-3 reads, *"In the beginning was the word and the word was with God. The same was in the beginning with God. Through him all thing were made. Without him was not anything made that was made. In him was life, and that life was the light of men."*

This tells me that Jesus Christ and God are one, in the beginning was the word and the word was God.

God word is the bread of life and in his word is where you will find life. Mark 8:35 says, *"For whosoever will lose their life for my sake and the gospel's the same shall save it."*

That means whosoever holds on to this life, doing everything under the sun that is pleasing to him or her, rather it be a sinful life style or just pleasure of the world.

In the end you will lose your place in the kingdom of God and also loses your soul to the devil.

But those who give up many of the things they like doing in life. And start doing the things of God, and what he love.

Then you have a place in the kingdom of God reserved especially for you, and your souls shall be saved eternal with God.

I read over in the book of James where he once said if you believe like you should then why do you behave like you shouldn't.

To believe also means to have faith.

Hebrews 10:22 tells us *"To draw near with a pure heart in full assurance of faith, having our hearts sprinkled from an evil conscience, and our bodies wash with pure water."*

Verse 23, *"Let us hold fast the profession of our faith without wavering, for he is faithful that promised."*

Verse 24, *"Let us consider one another to provoke unto love and good works."*

Verse 25, *"Not forsaking the assembling of ourselves together as the manner of some is; but exhorting one another and so much the more as ye see the day approaching."*

Rom. 12:9 says *"Let love be without dissimulation abhor that which is evil, cleave to that which is good."*

Verse 10 *"Be kindly and affectionate one to another, roman with brotherly love in honour preferring one another"*

Verse 12:11 reads *"Not slothful in business fervent in spirit; serving the lord"*

Verse 12:12, *"Rejoicing in hope; patient in tribulation, continuing instant in prayer."*

Roman 12:1-2 says *"I beseech you breathen by the mercies of God that ye present your bodies a living sacrifice holy and acceptable unto God.*

Which is your reasonable service?"

Verse 12:2 *"And be not conform to this world; but be you be ye transform by the renewing of your mind, that ye may prove what is that good, and acceptable and perfect will of God."*

Present your bodies as a living sacrifice, Holy and acceptable unto God. It is not going to be as easy as it is to read it, you're going to have hard times and difficult days alone the way."

James 1-2 says *"Consider it pure joy my breathen whenever you face trails of many different situation,*

because you know that the testing of your faith develop perseverance, perseverance must finish it work so that you may be mature and complete, not lacking anything."

Meaning that you have grown up in the knowledge of God word and is now strong.

Meaning that now you will be able to walk this walk much better than before, without falling as much as we do.

If any of you lack wisdom he should ask God who gives generously to all without finding fault, and it will be given to him.

But when he asks he must believe and not doubt, ***because "He who doubts is like a wave of the sea driven with the wind. That man should not think he will receive anything from the lord; he is like a double minded man unstable in all his he does."***

Once we have come to believe in our hearts and know in our minds and have trusted in God throughout our life we should have no doubts in our mind knowing God has been good to us even in our wrong doings, and has love us unconditionally.

We should be fully persuaded in the lord, having no doubt that God is able to keep you from falling, he's able to do all things except fail, trust and obey God spoken word in plain view written just for you.

And you shall succeed as you continue to believe in his spoken word.

See then that you walk circumspectly not as fools, but as wise, redeeming the time because the days or evil.

Jimmy Jordan - The Messenger

May you continue succeed to achieve that which ye believe in. If you believe like you should why do you behave like you shouldn't.

You're Messenger Jimmy J.

Chapter Twenty-Seven

Walking Worthy

Praise the Lord!

To walk worthy you must be ready to put up a fight; and contain your lustful desires, reframing yourselves from doing wrong.

To walk worthy means we as Christian must be willing to put down certain things in our lives that we know is not pleasing to God and be ready to walk in a way that pleases the father in heaven.

To walk worthy one must trust and obey God's word. To walk worthy one must believe, and strive to achieve that which ye believe in. To walk worthy one must have faith, it's going to be times when you experience hardship, it's going to be times when the devil put devilish thoughts on your minds to make it seem like God is not there, but just as sure as you have hair on your head, I want you to know and believe He's there.

Sometimes bad things happen in your life and things just do not seems to be going right for you.

The devil will try to shake your faith so that you may become a child of the devil, to walk worthy does not comes easy one must fight to walk worthy and upright, to stay on the battlefield, do God's will stay connected to the Father in heaven, and be a child of God.

To walk worthy, one is going to need some authentic faith, meaning genuine, we all know genuine means to be real, real genuine faith does not snap when it is stretch to the breaking point.

That's the kind of faith one must possess, because without it you are going to find yourself falling short, if you posses that real genuine faith, that will help you in many different ways.

Eph. 4:17 says, *"This I therefore, and testify in the lord that ye walk not as other gentiles walk, in the vanity of their minds, having their understanding darkened, being alienated from the life of God through the ignorance that is in them, because of the blindness in their heart."*

To walk as other gentiles in the vanity of their minds is not walking worthy, they walk with Christ was in vain: without success, to walk in vain is to walk unholy, to walk unholy is being alienated from the life of God, to be alienated from God is to be separated from God, and that's a very dangerous thing to do, it's a terrible and sad way to be, being separated from God.

To be separated from God is to be joining with the devil, to be join with the devil is walking in darkness, when you're walking in darkness you're not able to see the kingdom of God and all the things he has plan for you.

Eph. 5:1-4 says, *"Be ye therefore followers of God as dear children: and walk in love, as Christ also hath given himself for us an offering and as a sacrifice to God as dear children: And walk in love as Christ hath loved us as he hath given himself as a sweet smelling savour."*

Eph. 5:3 says, *"But fornication, and all uncleanness, or covetousness, let it not be once name among you as becoming saints; Neither filthiness nor foolish talking, nor jesting which are not convenient; but rather given thanks."*

Eph. 5:5 says, *"For this ye know that no whore monger nor unclean person, nor covetous man who is an idolater hath any inheritance in the Kingdom of Christ and of God."*

Eph. 5:8 tell us *"For ye were sometime darkness but now ye are light in the lord; walk as children of the light."* Eph 6:10-13 *say, "Finally my brethren, be strong in the lord, and in the power of his might." Put on the full amour of God that ye may be able to stand against the wiles of the devil. For our struggle is not against flesh and blood, but against rulers against authorities, against the power of this dark world, and against spiritual forces of evil in the heavenly realms. Wherefore put on the whole armor of God so when the day of evil comes you may be able to withstand in the evil day, and having done all to stand."*

Stand firm then, with the belt of truth buckle around your waist, with the breast plate of righteousness in place, and your feet shod with the readiness that comes from the gospel of peace.

In addition to all this take up the shield of faith, with which you can extinguish all the flaming arrows of the evil one. Take the helmet of salvation and the sword of the spirit which is the word of God.

And pray in the spirit on all occasions with all kinds of prayers and requests, with this in mind be alert and always keep praying for all saints. Now that's walking worthy and ready for war.

To walk worthy one should have a willingness to serve and help others in need.

To walk worthy one must be willing to go that extra mile to seek God; to walk worthy one must be willing to die daily for the love of God, both physically and spiritually.

To walk worthy one must live by God's word and be willing to share God's word with other believer and non believers.

God word is able to save your soul and make you whole. Hebrew 4:12 tells us *"For the word of God is quick and powerful, and sharper than any two edge sword, piercing even the dividing of asunder of souls, and spirit and of the joints and marrow, and is a discerner of thoughts and intents of the heart."*

There is power in the word of God, God word will lead you and guild you to help you walk worthy. I beseech you brethren and sister that ye walk worthy, and continue to strive for righteousness sake that you be found worthy because if you do not it's going to be outstanding price to pay.

I suggest that you walk worthy my brethren and sisters because the ones who do not will be punish.

2 Thessalonians 1:9-11 say *"Who shall be punish with everlasting destruction from the presence of the lord, and from the glory of his power: verse 1:10 When he shall come to be glorified in his saints, and be admired*

in that day. Wherefore also we pray always for you that our God would count you worthy of this calling, and fulfill all good pleasure of his goodness and the work of faith with power."

2 Thessalonians 2:1, *"Now we beseech brethren, by the lord Jesus Christ, and our gathering together unto him. That ye be soon not shaken in mind, or be troubled, neither by spirit, nor by word, nor by letter, as from us, as the day of Christ is at hand."*

Verse 13, *"But we are bound to give thanks always to God for you. Brethren beloved of the lord, because God hath from the beginning chosen you to salvation through sanctificitation of the spirit and belief of the truth."*

Verse 14 *"Whereunto he who called you by our gospel to the obtain of our lord Jesus Christ. Steadfast meaning to stand firm and hold the traditions which ye been taught rather by word or epistle."* Now our lord Jesus Christ and God, even our father given us everlasting consolation and good hope through grace, comfort your hearts and establish you in every good work.

2Thessalonain 3:6 *"Now we command you brethren that ye withdraw yourself from every brother that walketh disorderly among you, may you yourselves walk worthy"*

Amen. God bless and keep you.

You're Messenger Jimmy J.

WELCOME
Crusade for Christ
Church Hon
Sunday School 9:30 am
Worship Service
Wed. Bible Service
Minister Earl Jordan,
Whosoever will, let Him

Chapter Twenty-Eight

God Way Is The Best Way

Praise the Lord Believers and non-believers. God Ways is the best way.

He knows what's best for me and he knows what's best for you

He already knows which way we are traveling, He knows where we been and He knows all about our sins. He knows how many of our lives been toning apart following the ways of Satan.

Many of us today are living our life just the way he wants us to, he likes the way men and women, boy and girls, are living a life of been misused abused, and taking mind altering drugs keeping their minds confused.

He loves the way people of the world display bad minds and negative behavior, hateful attitudes towards one another, he likes the way people shove love in the closest were it is contained and other are not able to see it or grab a hold of it.

He likes the way we tare each other down, instead of lifting up one another, he likes the way we steal from one another hurt one another, and even kill each other.

Satan loves the way we disobey and stay frustrated, hesitating on doing what's right.

Many of us have lost our way in life and have a hard time making up their minds in which way shall they go, who shall they serve God or Satan, may you choose the right one who will lead you the right way.

God way is the best way if we follow His ways we find ourselves doing better, you will find yourselves treating other people better, and you will find more peace and happiness in your life as you walk down the road of righteousness.

I found out my ways cause me to repeat things over and over causing me to spend money, time and time again.

But if I would have let God lead me and do things his way, I could have saved money and time, friendships, fights, arrests court charges and fines, even my life and my mind.

Lets us not be in a hurry to do things Satan way, let us take our time and do things God way.

I found out his way is the best way, be obedient to God Spoken word and do things his way.

John 14:5 *"Thomas saith unto him Lord we know not whether thou goes; and how can we know the way; Jesus saith I am the way the truth and the life, no man can come unto the father but by me. Jesus is our way."*

When your way gets hard look to Jesus, he will be right there, when it seems like you can't find your way in life look to Jesus he will be right there. When your money is short and you barely have food to eat look to Jesus when you need clothes to wear or shoes to put on your feet look to Jesus He will supply all your needs, feel free to call on him at any time.

God's Spoken Word In Plain View

Because he said in his word to cast all your burdens on him as well your cares and concerns

God way is the best way, he woke us up this morning and started us on our way, He showed us which way to go through his son Jesus who died for us we are to do as he do.

He said let this mind be in you that is in Christ Jesus so we may think as he think, he also said be ye holy as I am holy

May we look through the eyes of Jesus and see thing and people the way he see things and people.

If you tired of the bad ways of the world, and the way of the world is not working for you, and have disappointed you, let you down, beat you down and people misused you and abused you.

Why not try Jesus and do things God way, his way is the best way when you have tried to find happiness in the night club, and love on the date-line yet and still you have failed to find true happiness and real love, try Jesus, when your life is a mess and peace is far away, you're not able to find love, happiness or peace. Suddenly Satan whisper in your ear follow me I know where you can find peace, love, and happiness all in one place mixed up in one bottle, and rolled up in one sheet of paper.

Many are following the ways of Satan to the liquor store, dope house, strip clubs, and many more avenues that leads unto a dead end road of darkness and destruction.

Drinking the devil juice and listening to his lies, trying to find a peace of mind, love and happiness.

When the devil juice is gone, and all of your friends are gone home.

And you find yourself alone thinking about how disrespectable you been an d the money you spent trying to have a good time, following Satan after all you spent on having a so called good time, you find yourselves still looking for true love real happiness and peace.

Seeing that you're not able to find the love you want at home, nor can you find in the streets. Neither can you find the peace you need nor the happiness you deserve.

Your minds is constantly looking for fulfillment, and companionship, your hearts is starving for real love and happiness do not give up, just try to do things God way, and you will find true love abiding in your hearts, peace and happiness will be flowing through your minds when you do things God way, you will find yourselves beings bless.

James 3:9 reads "Therewith bless we God, and therewith curse we men even the Father; which are made after the similitude of God."

Verse 10 says *"Out of the same mouth proceeded blessing and cursing*, my brethren these things ought not to be, if we are children of God we are to be a blessing to God and other and not curse to yourself and others.

By rehearsing evil seeking to do wrong following Satan going the wrong way, lets us make a U-turn, turn around and follow after righteousness.

Do things God way his way is the best way, if you're lost and need some direction pick up the holy bible.

Which the basis instruction before leaving earth, and our road map to life, while we're on this side, let us strive to get it right before we cross over to the other side's get your house in order now and your business fix with Jesus.

So when you take your flight over on the other side you will be traveling to higher heights.

And not going down to the lower parts deep below the grounds were Satan and his demons dwell in hell.

Through the outer darkness where nobody wants to go. I do not want to go there, and I do not know anyone who would like to go there, even though there is some who love darkness better than light.

But for me I want to be able to see where I am going, I travel in darkness many years and lost many of valuable things, I myself was lost in sin.

Following after Satan and doing the things he would have me to do, but God brought me out of darkness into the marvel's light so I can see, now I'm following after Christ Jesus, walking in the light doing the things of God and all what he would have me to do I found out that God way is the best way.

He's been better to me than I been to myself, he gave me spiritual insight, he showed me love, gave me peace, protected me in the streets fed me at home, by providing food for me to eat.

Jimmy Jordan - The Messenger

He's been a way maker when it seems like there was no way and I couldn't make it, but somehow I made it, some kind of way I made through Jesus is the way that made it all possible for you and me to be alive today.

You're Messenger Jimmy J.

Chapter Twenty-Nine

Dying To The Sinful Things Of This World

We all know that dying means to stop living, so dying to the sinful things of this world, simply means to stop living a sinful life,

Lord has mercy on all these different area of sin in our lives'.

I know we all struggle with some sort of sin in our life, some may ask the question what is sin

Webster tells me that sin is 1.-action that breaks a religious law 2-an action that is felt to be bad sin is wrong doing, evil thinking.

God knows the whole world is struggling with sin, that's why He sent his own son Jesus Christ into the world to die for the sins of the world so we might live.

In order for us to live a life with Christ we must die, when I say we must die I mean die to sin Jesus died once for all, but the life he lives, he lives unto God in the same manner we must live our life unto God.

Count yourselves dead to sin but alive to God in Christ Jesus.

To be dead to sin we must die daily, stop doing the things that displease God day by day, little by little, one must focus on his wrongs and start correcting his wrongs into rights so he or she may overcome the things that Satan brings into play to overpower you each and every day.

To be dead to sin one must stop inviting sin to come into your life one must stop making sin welcome and stop trying to satisfy the desires of sin and shut the door on sin, and let sin know I don't like you or what you do. Your not welcome here anymore lock the door put the change on it and secure it some more, Satan comes to steal kill and destroy, one must not only guard the doors of his house to keep the enemy from getting in one must also guard the doors of their heart protect your hearts by studying God word and put on the shield of faith that will protect you from all the fiery darts aiming to Peirce your hearts.

One must be willing to fight and die to sin by giving up anything that displeases God.

To come alive in Christ, one must open up the doors of his heart and welcome Christ into your life make him feel at home, in order to do that we must decrease so that Christ can increase let us get rid of the things in our life that we do not need and make room for God and the son of man; better known as Jesus Christ whom we need in our life very much.

Let him filled us with his love, joy, peace, and his spirit, to come alive in Christ one must live a spirited filled life that pleasing to God almighty.

Let us strive to continue to walk in the spirit. Roman 4:51-2 reads *"Therefore being Justified by faith we have peace with God through our Lord Jesus Christ; by whom also we have access by faith into grace wherein we stand and rejoice in hope of the glory of God."*

We cannot stand before God full of sin, if we plan on making it into Heaven Many of our minds and hearts polluted with sin, and we need to ask God to renew our minds and give us a clean heart.

Let us stop living unto the ways of Satan, doing his dirty work, hurting one another, destroying ourselves with drugs and alcohol, that the devil used to keep our minds confused off track and defocus taking his posing and drinking the devil juice, living unrighteous lives' doing evil things pleasing Satan and displeasing God.

Using all sort of profanity and evil communication exploiting ourselves sexually, many of our minds are filled with dirty thoughts and the majority of us are acting on those bad minds and carrying out those dirty thoughts, keeping ourselves bound and burden down.

Most of us have been serving Satan for far too long, and it's time that we stop.

And start serving God, by starting to die to the sinful things of this world. And give your minds and time to God, start living a righteous life unto God. He loves us and cares for us, He keeps us safe, and gives us his blessing as well as our hearts desires, and he cleans us up when we have made a mess of our self from living dirty sinful lives.

He gives us a better mind time and time again, let us evaluate our lives and see who deserve our time, mind and the life we live.

Amen. May God bless you!

You're Messenger Jimmy J.

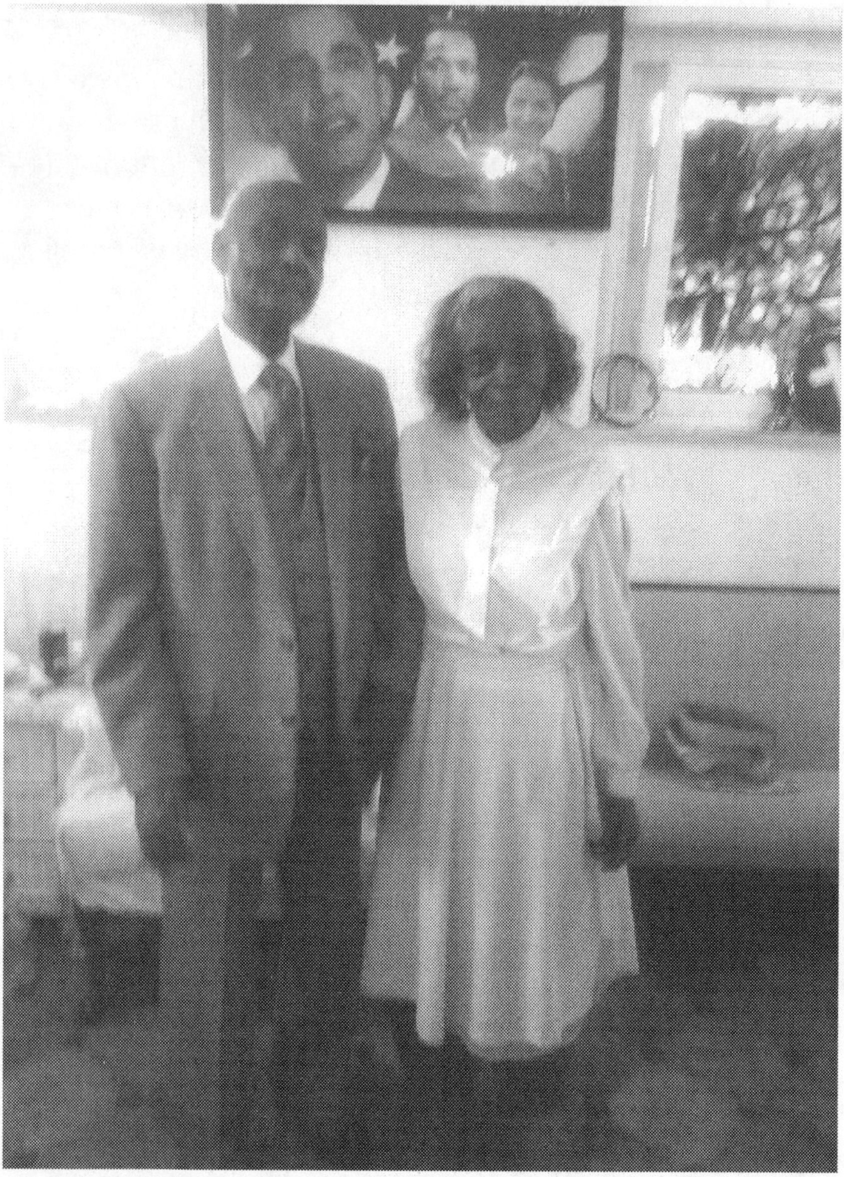

Chapter Thirty

Take Nothing For Granted

Praise the Lord Saints! And thank Him for second chances. I thank him for sparing my life.

God has gave many of us second chances over and over, and some of us still have yet to learn how to live, most of us are quick to take risks and do things to harm ourselves and do things that will also make other people hurt you the majority of us act on things before thinking about the things they do and the consequences we must face, because we gamble with our lives and take too many chances, and take advantage of God love for us.

God is the lover of our soul, and has purchased us with His blood, so you see we really don't own ourselves.

God owns our bodies and we belong to Him. The life that we gamble with it is really not ours to play with.

Even though we do all manner of things, not really concerned about the way we live and the one who gave us life, but let us think twice how precious life really is and stop being so quick to take risks, and do all manner of things by trying to gain a lot (which will not last long) with a little smarts, trickery, and pizzazz.

God's Word said *"Let us be slow to anger but swift to hear."* God word says *"For what does a man profit, if he shall gain the whole world and lose his soul?"*

Matthew 26:25, *"For whosoever will save his life shall loose it: and whosoever shall lose his life for my sake shall find it."*

For those who don't understand the meaning of that saying, it means those who gamble with their life, do all manner of things, and cleave to the pleasures of this world unlike those who give up all the worldly things, and sinful pleasures of this world and cleave to God, these shall find life because God will bless you and give you the desires of thine heart and you shall be able to live a peaceful and prosperous life.

Let us redeem the time, because the days are evil, so while the blood still runs warm in our veins we need to strive to do better and fulfill ye the joy of the lord, and if you still want to gamble and take chances, throw it all down on the line for Jesus if you do this, He is a sure win.

Jesus spoke and said, and I will give unto thee the keys of the Kingdom of Heaven: and whatsoever thou shalt bind on earth shall be bound in Heaven: and whatsoever thou shalt loose on, earth shall be loosed in Heaven, Free your mind and redeem the time. **Psalms 103:4 "Who redeemed thy life from destruction who crowneth thee with love and kindness and tender mercies".**

Thank God for second chances and redeeming the lost, I'm glad that I found Jesus because I truly was lost just like many of you are who play games with Satan gambling with your lives and losing all you have.

When the stakes are high we play to win, but let us be mindful of the game we are playing, and who we are playing with, if you are playing games with Satan; let me give you a heads up and let you know the steaks are always high He is going to make it good to you and give you double or nothing.

I played games with the devil and lost, so I'm helping you win by letting you know what is in his hand: he has 2 queens, a jack, black deuce, Ace and a Joker. He will play his queen of diamonds first, he will send her to lure you in through her shining, sparkling, and enticing ways, and then he'll come back in a different suit with another queen, the queen of hearts which aim to steal your love so he then will have your heart.

Next he'll come back in that same suit with the a little black deuce trying to trick us with his trickery to make it seem like we have the upper hand, when all the time he has a plan and an ace in the hole to steal your soul.

He will do it so slick he will play the jack of all trades, then he will send jack over to help you to make you lower your guards down, but instead of jack helping you. He comes and hurt you and beat you down and takes what is yours.

But after you start to recover from a few rounds of the beat down, you begin to play again, and just when you thought things was getting better he'll throw down the ace in the hole which is used to strip you out of anything he may allow you to win, right before he plays the joker to end the game.

(Which is you) whom he was looking and watching you play a losing game; because he thinks he is in control, but that is exactly where he went wrong and lost the game, because he is **not** in control.

God is in control and he has the whole kingdom in his hands. He has all the kings, queens, aces in the hole, he is the real lover of your soul, He has the Jack of all trades and army of soldiers and the whole world is in His hands.

If one wishes to win at the Game of Life, he must get on God's side and strive for righteousness, keeping your head up, when the ways of the world seem to bring you down. Remember: **"troubles don't last always and you are more than a conqueror."**

Thorough the strength of Jesus you can conquer many of things with faith in God and believing in His son who has already won the victory over our lives.

Jesus has already made the pathway for us to escape, all we hath to do is follow in His footsteps and we can also have the victory in Jesus, and victory over things in our own lives that may come against us to bring us down.

He said in His word, **"if I be for you who can be against us?"** Life is a gamble but if you roll with Jesus you will win the game.

It is plain to see if you roll with Jesus life will be easier, but if you continue to gamble and play games with Satan a lot of valuable things will be lost: money, diamonds, and gold rings. And many things.

He will even take your self esteem, hopes and dreams, and everything in-between.

If you play with him long enough he will make you lose your mind and go insane.

It behooves me to tell you Satan is here to stay and he will always be ready to play and remember the game don't change only the faces of the players, your chance for winning is slim to none with Satan.

If you want to win in the game of life, then one must wake up and put on your war clothes, dance to a different beat on the other side of the street that what is one must do, make your move by switching avenues and play the game by God's rules and you won't lose.

The game make take longer to win and it might even get bored but in the end you'll win by a land slide without a doubt meaning it was a wipe out and now you are on your way to the top and win it all from city to city state to state, playing with the high roller in the big leagues in big places sit at the table with the most high, think of the big places as a place in your mind, and look at the table as your heart.

Keep God on your mind and Jesus in your heart at all times.

Thank God for second chances, because many of you could have been dead and gone, from the first time they decided to go and do some wrong or from their first heart attack or stroke or maybe being diagnosed with some sickness such as cancer, or sugar diabetes. There are many reasons and answers as to why one was not given a second chance, but thank God for given us a second chance Amen.

You're Messenger Jimmy J.

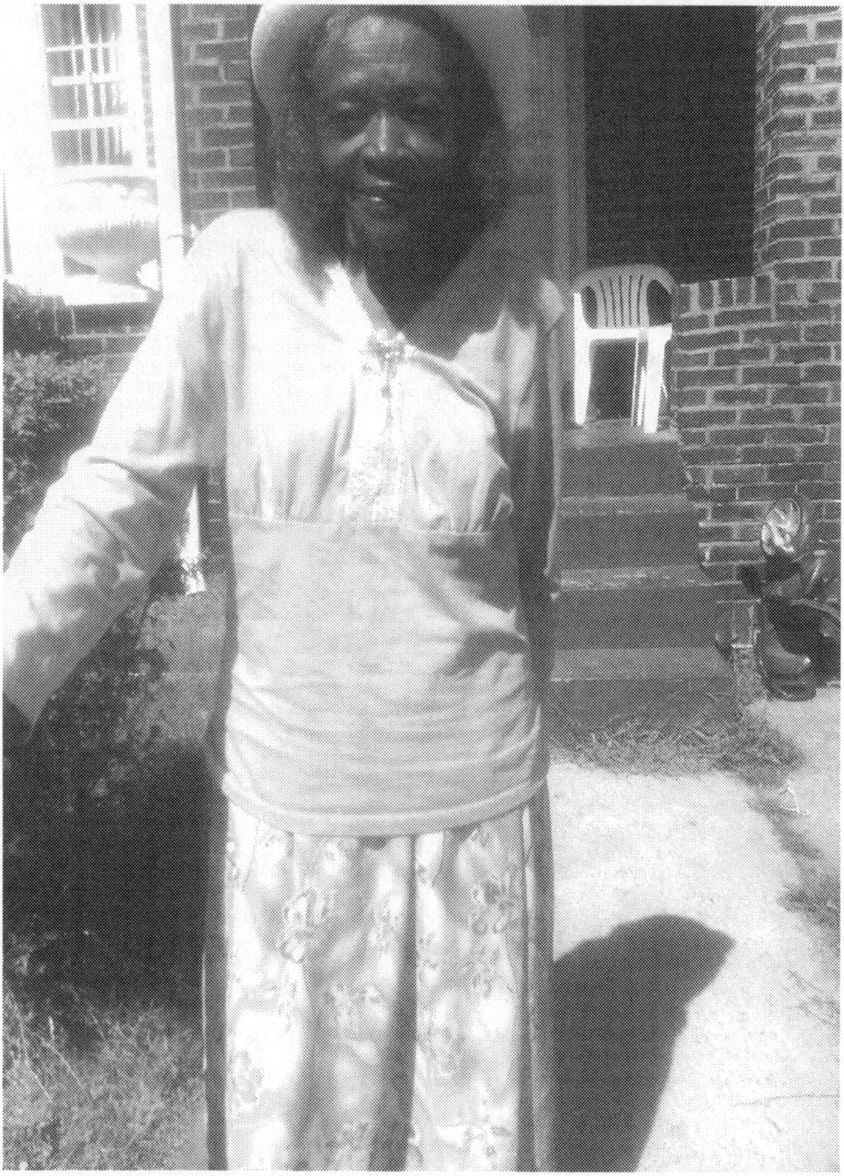

Chapter Thirty-One

If we love God like we say we do why we do the things He hates

Praise the lord saints, May we continue in his word, and abide in him.

If we say we love God, why do we do the things he hates? He said in his word if you love me: keep my commandments.

If you love the lord thy God, let us try to hit it a little harder to do the things he say.

He said in his word follow me for am the truth, the way and the life: Jesus is the light of the world in him there's no darkness.

The light of Christ will shine on those spot in your life. His word will wash those dark spots clean and bring you out of darkness into the marvelous light.

He said in his word if you keep your minds stayed on me our give you peace; praise God, thank you Jesus: there's nothing worth more than having a peace of mind, Jesus said in his word if you believe in me, you should also believe in my father abide in me, I will abide in you.

He also said let us work while it is day, for when night set in we become older, weaker, and barely able to see, but the world is in such bad shape.

God can still use your voice, your mind, and some of your time. To be shared with those whom he cares for that maybe still lost.

God can still use you even in your old age.

He said in his word if you do my will I will bless you and pour out blessings on you, so abundantly you won't have room enough to store them. God is in the blessing business, he will bless you and supply all of your needs, through his riches and glory, God can use all of us even in our old age.

He used Noah to build an ark to save himself and his family from the flood that destroyed the world

He also used him to save the animals of every kind. And used him to warn the people to let them know it's going to rain, trying to save them because a flood is coming. He used old man Noah and his family to repopulate and create a brand new world.

God can use you no matter who you are, no matter what age you may be, he can use you. He used the foolish people of the world and made them to become wise.

If we say we love the lord like we say we do let him use us for his glory, and the building of his kingdom. Not always just for self, our place of business, our home, our comfort zone if we say we love the lord like we say we do let us spread that love to others.

If we say we love the lord like we say we do, why do we harbor so much hatred in our hearts toward one another? And hurt each other.

He said in his word what you do to the least one of my children you do the same unto me.

If we choose not to hurt God, let us not hurt one another. He also said love that we have for yourself and other's will cleanse us from all unrighteousness, God's love will mend broken hearts back together again.

God loves us unconditional, no matter how wrong we been, he still shows us love no matter what condition our minds are in.

God is able to lift the weight of the world off your shoulders, and free your mind from been burden down, and let you find peace, joy, happiness, and some time spent with him.

Many of us today say we love the lord, but never bring him anything.

If you love the lord like you say you do let us offer him something, if nothing but some thanks unto the lord. Because he has been good to all of us.

Let us give some of our time to serve and worship him.

Let us give our mind to study his word, let us give ear to hear the teaching been taught and take heed to the doctrine we already heard.

Many of us say we love the lord but never give him anything. No money, none of your time, no praise's, no prayers, no sincerity, no people for the building of the kingdom, and no repentance.

But lets start giving something to the lord, if we love him like we say we do show him that you love him and believe in his word put your trust in him because he able to fix anything that you maybe going through.

I know he was able to pick me up when I was down, let him know lord I know you able to keep me when I don't want to be kept, let him know you know all power is in his hands and, I know you able to hold back the enemy from trying to take what's mine many of us say we love the lord and barely know him, many of us say we love the lord, and hardily ever walked with him, very seldom talk to him.

Rarely listen to what he got to tell us, the majority of us are disobedient to his teaching and we fall short in keeping his sayings, if we love the lord like we say we do.

Let us get to know him for our self, if we love the lord like we say we do. Let us talk to him on the regular basic, let our walk with him be longer, than from here to the corner.

Let us do better in our Christian walk, and go the distance traveling with Jesus all the way to the end.

Striving to be obedient and listening to what the spirit said unto the churches. We are the church the place we come to worship God in is just a church building pay more attention to the ones who are trying to help you, and show you, a better way in which we should live.

Many of us have had a hard time from listen to the devil, telling us to commit some sin, hurt a friend, hurt ourselves or hurt God through our disobedient, grieving

God spirit. If we love the lord like we say we do let us not serve Satan the devil more than we serve the lord.

The devil don't care about us, in fact he don't even like us, he's a hater he has no love for those who spent their whole life serving him, he has no love for them who bow down and worship him.

His only love is to hate, and create some mess that mess your life up and leave you clueless that he started it all.

The majority of all the problem and confusion comes from the father of lies. He only uses you to feed others a taste of what's cooking down below.

He's preparing his favorite meal made with hatred and mixed with poison served daily with a fresh dish of death made per order just for you.

But we do not hath to eat what the devil is serving, because it's no good, and out of date, the food he's serving is gone pass its expiration date.

It is no good for you it will mess you up.

But if you come out from among sitting in the devil's kitchen and look up to Jesus he'll lead you to a far better life and peace shall be served all day.

Drinks are free, once you have tasted the food from this place and have ate from the table of God.

And drunk from the spiritual fountain of everlasting water, your souls and minds shall be filled with the love of God, and you shall never thirst again.

Psalm 107:2-9, **"Let the redeemed say so whom he hath redeemed from the hand of the enemy; and gather them** *from the east, from the west from the north, and from the south. They found no city to dwell in. hungry and thirsty they souls fainted in them. Then they cried unto the lord in their troubles and he delivered them out of their distresses and led them forth by the right way; that they may go to a city of habitation."*

Oh those men would praise the lord for his goodness.

For he sanctified the longing soul and fills the hungry soul with goodness. His word will revive you his spirit will fill you with power, love, wisdom, and strength.

His word will keep you alive. Psalm 111:1-9 *"Praise ye the lord, I will praise the lord with my whole heart, in the assembly of the upright, and the congregation."*

Verse 2, *"The works of the lord are great, sought out of all them that have pleasure there in."*

Verse 3, *"His work is honorable and glorious: and his righteousness endures forever."*

Verse 4 *"He hath made his wonderful works to be remembered: the lord is gracious and full of compassion."*

Verse 5, *"He has given meat unto them that fear him: he will ever be mindful of his covenant."*

Verse 6 *"He has shown his people the power of his work that he may give them the heritage of the heathen."*

A heathen is a person who does not know or worship the God of the bible.

God has shown his powers to many who did not know him, and punish them for their ungodly ways to let them know there is a God, and we must be mindful of his covenant.

Verse 7, **"The works of his hands are verity judgment; all his commandment or sure."** He has many opportunity of work available to us.

He will be judging us according to the work we do.

He's the one and only true God and judge of the world.

Let us go on talking about the commandments of the lord. Verse 8, reads **"They stand fast forever and ever, and are done in truth and uprightness."**

The commandments of the lord will stand forever for they uphold the truth of God's word.

And will be done by all those who walk upright.

Verse 9, reads **"He sent redemption unto his people: he hath commanded his covenant for ever: Holy and reverend is his name."**

He sent his son into the world to redeem the lost, Jesus Christ the savior of the world brought redemption to a lost and dying world through his blood when he died on the cross at cal very.

If we love the lord Jesus Christ why do we do the things he hates, if we love the lord thy God why do we do the things he commanded us not to do. Help us lord to get our minds right and show more love toward the lord thy God.

He said in his word if you love me keep my commandments,"

God is love many of us say we love god but continually to do the things he hate.

He also said in world over in 1 John 4:20-21 *"If a man says I love God and hated his brother, he is a lyre: for he that loved not his brother whom he hath seen, how can he love God whom he hath not seen."*

21 say *"And this commandment have we from him, that he who loved God, loved his brother also."*

Let us show our love toward God by loving one another and helping each other.

Let us remember love covers a multitude of sin, show love and not hate.

1 Cor. 13:1-2 tells us *"Though I speak with the tongues of men and of angels and have not charity I am become as sounding brass or a tinkling cymbal. And though I have the gift of prophecy and understand all mysteries, and all knowledge: and though I have all faith so I could remove mountains and have not charity, am nothing."*

That the ends of this message of if you say you love the lord thy God why do you do the things he hates. May God bless you, hope something was said to help you show more love.

                    You're Messenger Jimmy J.

Chapter Thirty-Two

Stand

Praise the lord and thank him for giving us strength to stand: thank him for allowing us another chance to stand for righteousness as we walk this Christian walk.

When our light become dim and our way become dark help us to stand and harkens unto the voice of the lord.

Our minds are burdened down confusion and worry. Regulate our minds lord and help us stand. When we become weak make us strong and help us stand. Even though we already know sometimes we are going to be made to fall.

Because the devil will throw many stumbling blocks our way to make us fall, were going to see many of side shows to defocus us so we can take our eyes off Jesus and focus on the world and the worldly things that goes on; they're going to be much kayos and confusion, corruption, and destruction in the world that we live in that has a way of creeping in our lives to bring us down and make us fall.

Thank God for Jesus who is able to pick you up and help you to stand.

Help us lord to stand, Let us strive and walk upright let us not walk sideways, crooked, or backwards, with one foot in the grave and one foot on solid ground.

Let us walk with both feet on solid ground of the sure foundation of Jesus Christ.

The foundation of Jesus Christ is strong, it's wide and long made to last and stretch from everlasting to everlasting; and holds millions of people that stand up and walk with Jesus, the foundation he laid for you and me is strong.

Stand for truth, stand for righteousness, stand for peace, stand with love, and stand up for the one who stood for you: that someone is Jesus whose righteousness still stand today.

Stand with the one who love you, stand for the one who cares for you, stand for the one who deserve the honor and praises due unto him.

Stand for Jesus because he the reason why were standing on our own two feet.

Stand boldly stand with confidence trusting and believing in God's word having no doubt knowing that God is able to bring you out, I know for myself God is able because he brought me a mighty long way, a he brought through danger seen, and unseen, he brought me over the bridge of troubled waters and carry me to a safe place, he lifted my head from sinking in sin, he rescue me and saved my life so I can live again.

He was there when I was not there for myself; he caught me when I let myself go.

He came to my rescue when he heard my cry, thank you Jesus for letting me live and not die.

Thank the Lord Jesus for his love mercy and Grace, Thank him day in and day out, thank him in the morning, and thank him late at night.

For it was his mercy that kept us and his grace that saved us, Jesus love for the world freed us?

Eph. 6:13 reads *"Wherefore take unto you the whole amour of God that ye may be able to stand in the evil day, and having done all to stand,"*

Verse 14 says *"Stand therefore having your loins girt about with truth, and having on the breastplate of righteousness."*

Your cover with the word of truth, your shield, when you put on the breastplate of righteousness it is much more powerful than a bullet proof vest, which is unable to keep you safe and protect you from a bullet to the head.

I am not just saying something to amuse you I'm speaking from experience. I myself, the Messenger Jimmy Jordan took a bullet to the back of my head, and was made to fall, left for dead.

But today I stand because I trusted and depended and on Jesus to save me, had I would have trusted in a bullet proof vest to save me I would still be laying down, but because I trusted in Jesus He picked me up when I was down and help me to stand.

Praise the Lord I thank him for his goodness now I can run on and tell other about his goodness.

Let us run on and tell other about the Gospel of peace, take off your walking shoes and put on your running shoes, stand for God and spread the good news.

Put on your running shoes and let God used your legs and feet to go see about others and help one another, let him use your mouth to speak of his goodness.

If God been good to you run on and tell others about his goodness.

Verse 16 says *"Above all taking the shield of faith, where with ye shall be able to quench all the fiery darts of the wicket, out of everything you take alone with you take your faith in God with you, for it is by faith that you are saved; faith without works is dead."*

He said in his word show me your faith and I will show you my works by faith.

Eph. 6:17 says *"And take the helmet of salvation, and the sword of the spirit, which is the word of God."*

Verse 18 reads *"Praying always with all prayers and supplication in the spirit, and watching thereunto with all saints lets us stand in the gap for others who have lost their way in life."*

And is unable to read the road map that leads to life.

Let us stand for the babies and the younger generation that look upon older adults for guidance, let us stand on the promise of God.

Let us not sit down on God 'word, nor should we continue to lay in sin if we have God word in us.

Let us stand and carry God word unto those who need to be fed.

There's many of starving people hungry for God word who need to be fed, may somebody be led to feed somebody God word anybody carrying God word, can feed to everybody whom they see in need of it.

Stand in for a friend who may be sinking in sin.

Stand for your mother the first one who discovered you were being born, stand for your sister and brothers that may see something in you, that will show them the light of Christ, to be able to see how to walk this walk this walk, and live down here in this world without falling as much as we do. Stand for your father for it was him who help made you who you are.

Stand when your back is against the wall when the devil comes to attack you, don't run, and stand your grounds.

When he say jump don't say how high, stomp that devil under your feet and say bye-bye, do not be his puppet on a string who he winds up and plays with your mind building you up to commit some sin.

He winds you up only to see himself throw you down, and convince you to do more sin and throw you down again.

Do not be his yo-yo doing things God said no-no that not for you to do.

Stand down on the things the devil wants you to do and stand up for the things God wants you to do.

Verse 14, *"Let all things be done with charity, be real and do all things in love."*

Philippians 4:1 reads *"Therefore my brethren dearly beloved and longed for, my joy and crown, so stand fast in the Lord my dearly beloved."*

If anyone wish to make it into the kingdom of heaven and long to see Jesus fulfill ye the joy of the Lord.

If ye wish to receive a crown of righteousness stand fast, and walk upright. To receive a crown of life, we must first give our life to Jesus, then we must live a life that's pleasing in his eye sight; so when the day of judgment come and we all must come before the God and the son of man; may we hear those uplifting words being spoken unto us saying well done son you being faithful over a few things come on up higher and I'll make you ruler of many.

When we stand before God and the son of man may we be in right standard with God.

Because all the begging and pleading, dropping to your knee's will not get you into heaven.

Now is the time to drop to your knees and plead your case and ask God for forgiveness, repent for all the wrongs you done.

Today is the day of repentance tomorrow is not promise to us.

Therefore let us strive to get it right today.

If you wish to stand and not fall get on your knees and talk to Jesus, I heard it's been said it's hard for a man to fall when he's down on his knees.

When you get down on your knees and praying talk to God and let him know what you stand in need of and what's standing in your way, say look Lord I know I been wrong but I'm in need of your help, I need you to fix's it for me Jesus even though I know I messed it up."

Revelation 3:19-20 reads *"As many as I love, I rebuke and chasten; be zealous therefore and repent."*

For those who have a strong zeal to live for God repent of your wrongs and ask God for forgiveness get in right standard with God.

Verse 20 reads *"Behold—look I stand at the door and knock; if any man hear my voice, and open the door I will come into him and sup with him, and he with me."*

Jesus is knocking on the doors of many of our hearts today. Are we going to lay dormant while we're constantly being tormented by the devil? Are shall we stand up for God open the doors of your hearts and let him in.

Stand if you hath to stand alone, stand for something or you will fall for anything Satan brings. Stand faithful, honest, and true; let us not be so quick to disconnect ourselves from the righteousness of God.

Let us not lie to ourselves professing to be a Christian and living unrighteous and unholy lives, if you're doing wrong, and living displeasing lives unto God repent free your minds, let God cleanse your hearts. Stand in total freedom

You're Messenger Jimmy J.

Chapter Thirty-Three

Perishing from the lack of knowledge

Praise the lord, and thank him for all the God giving knowledge that's being giving to us all.

Jesus died and gave his life for all those who are dying in their sin, Pershing daily from the lack of knowledge and constant sin within the hearts of men, women boys and girls.

Too many people have died and left this world far too soon because of the lack of knowledge or because they did not use the knowledge that was giving them.

Too many people are still dying in their sin, perishing from the lack of knowledge.

It's sad to say but it will be more and more people dying and perishing in their sin every day.

It's sad to see those who are living dying spiritually, walking around dead sinking in sin, crying on the inside while their minds and bodies are being destroyed on the outside, anytime we stand on the outside of God will we stand a greater chance of being destroyed, losing our minds and bodies from the lack of knowledge.

God's Spoken Word In Plain View

We as the people of God have his knowledge living within us, but even though we know of him and have obtained much knowledge we ourselves sometimes fail to use the knowledge of what we know about God to help others.

Who needs our help, we as the people of God should share what we know to help other live and grow.

Many of us are lacking in giving the knowledge of God word to others, but when we do so it will help others grow more spiritually there shouldn't be nothing or no one more worthy of knowing, than knowing the word of God.

Because he's the one who is keeping us alive from day to day, its God word that strengthens us and his love that keeps us.

His word also keeps us abiding in his love as we strive for perfection study his word let it makes you wise.

So you may be doers of the word and not hearer only.

He said in his word do unto others as you would have them do unto you.

In other words if you do not want other people treating you bad, do not treat other people bad, if you want people to treat you good treat other people good.

He also said love ye one another, may you show love to others in the same manner as you would like them to show unto to you.

He said in his word over in the book of St. John 15:5, ***"I am the vine ye are the branches; He that abided in me,***

and I in him the same bringe'th forth much fruit; for without me ye can do nothing"

Jesus is the vine verse5 tells me that he is planted in me. He also said if ye abide in me and I in you as the vine cannot bear fruit of itself except ye abide in me, if we plan to grow spiritually we must abide in Jesus, to abide in Jesus we must walk upright and strive to live a righteous life.

We must dwell in his spirit both day and night we must also endure both misery and pain.

God is able to give you both peace and happiness; and comfort the hearts of those who are hurting and broken.

He said in his word ye are the branches; meaning that you are a part of the vine, you are extending from the vine, which is the mainline, Jesus is the mainline and roots that causes the branches to grow we the children of God are the branches that he is speaking about.

If we plan on growing physical financially, or spiritually we need to stay connected to the vine because without Jesus himself we can do nothing.

Many people of the world today have disconnected they self from the vine which is the mainline of power yet in still is trying to operate and function in life through their own strength, trying to succeed prosper, and grow, but Jesus said not so, If your prospering, growing, and succeeding in life it's because Jesus made it possible for you and allowed his blessing to fall down into your life.

Without Jesus we can do nothing, without Jesus we wouldn't even have a life.

Many people of the world is lacking Jesus in they life.

Fighting a losing battle, taking on a world of sin, kayos, and confusion, facing many trails and tribulation of a trouble world filled with pollution flooding the streets with evil and polluting the air with hatred.

Many find it hard to avoid the devils tactics attacking us daily beating us down leaving many of us daze, and bruise from a lack of knowledge, dying in our sins. Jesus is our way out turn to Jesus and he will bring you out of sin and give you life.

If we desire to survive in this mean and cruel world and want to stay alive we must stay connected to the vine.

Let us take heed to the knowledge of God word that's been giving to us so that we may do better.

St. John 15:6-7 says *"If a man abide not in me He is cast forth as a branch. And withered and men gather them and cast them into the fire,*

And they are burned."

In other words when you disconnect yourselves from the vine not only will you stop growing in the knowledge of God word you also cut off your power from that mainline of power.

And when men of evil devices come together against you to hurt you and cast you down into the evil Pitts of Satan world, you will be on your on fighting a losing battle, and you're bound to get burned.

But thanks be to God and his son Jesus Christ who spoke a word in St. John 15:7 and said *"If ye abide in me and my words in you ye shall ask what ye will, and it shall be done unto you."*

Verse 8 says *"Herein is Father Glorified that ye bear much fruit so ye s hall be called my disciples."* Verse 9 reads *"As the Father hath loved me so have I love you in my love."*

May we let the love of God continue to spread throughout our life. May God bless you, and may you rest from sin and work on get your mind right to live a righteous life in sight God.

Psalm 1:1-2 reads *"Blessed is the man walketh not in the counsel of the ungodly, nor sitted in the seat of the scornful."*

If you desire to be blessed of the lord live a blessed life and be a blessing to someone else.

2 reads *"But his delight is in the law of the lord; and in his law doth he meditate day and night."*

If you delight yourself in the Lord his word will shed some light on the darkness in your life and give you a better insight on life, many of those dark and cloudy days will become bright. The more you abide in his word, the less you will desire to do wrong.

Perishing from the lack of knowledge, the more you meditate on God's word the less stress you will have in your life.

2 Peter 3:9 reads *"The lord is not slack concerning his promise, as some men count slackness; but is longsuffering to us-ward not willing that any should perish, but that all should come to repentance."*

May we all repent of our wrongs and draw closer to God word to keep us from perishing from the lack of knowledge?

Hope something was said to help you become more knowledgeable of God's word Amen.

You're Messenger Jimmy J.

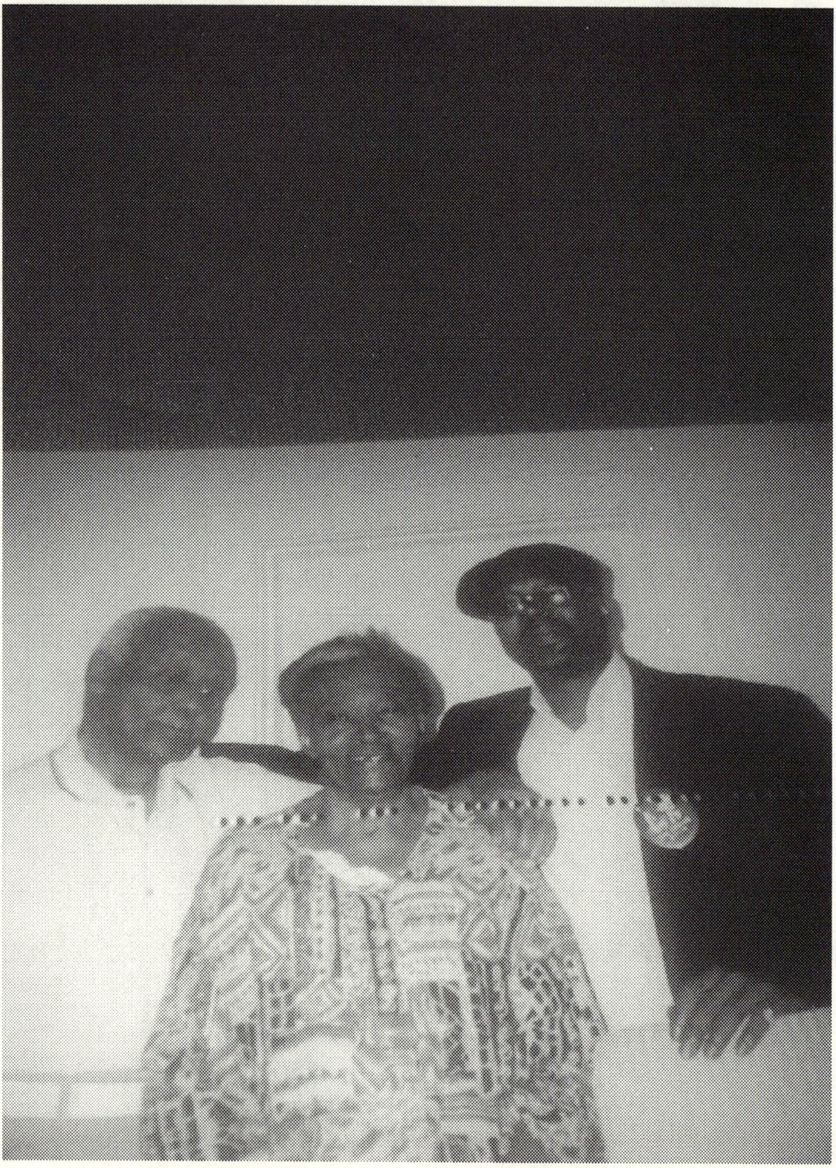

Chapter Thirty-Four

Pay day is coming

Praise the lord! May works we do be the type of works that's good and satisfactory to Him who gave us the job.

May the works we do be able to keep us even after we retire. I'm not just talking about going to a 9 to 5 job I'm talking about working for the Lord who wants labors to work for him in the vine yard 24/7 around the clock.

May you go the work for God and the retirement check you receive along with what's in your hearts will keep you from going down living in the Pitts of hell fire.

We all are going to retire, and one day our life will expire.

Pay day is coming soon get on board while there is still room, and receive the righteous pay God has in store for you.

Rev. 2:2 *"I know thy works and thy labor, and thy patience. And how thou cannot bear them which are evil; and thou hast tried them which say they are apostles and are not, and hast found them liars."*

God gave us this day so we can live, love, and play to enjoy life and stay faithful to him.

And help them that are down and lost, and trying to find their way in life.

Our days are filled with opportunities of giving help to those who are in need of some help.

Let us not take advantage of anyone's love, lets us advance to a higher level in our Christian walk with a stronger sincerity and security lock in to God keeping ourselves unspotted from the world and free from all the different impurity of sin.

Our days are filled with evil, and we never know what a day can bring us.

It can bring us life, peace, and happiness or heart aches and pain.

Jesus spoke a word to us in Matthew 6:11-13 through a word of prayer, asking the father in heaven ***"To give us this day our daily bread and forgive us of our debts as we forgive our debtors and lead us not into temptation. But deliver us from evil; for thine is the kingdom and the power and the glory forever Amen."***

Today is the day the Lord has made let us rejoice and be glad in it.

Let us not spend all our days with the devil that the Lord has given unto us to spend with him, and them who he loves.

May our days be well spent with the Lord, living to bring glory unto him and forgiving others for their wrongs.

Just as God has forgave us for our wrongs.

Everyday above ground is a good day, even though they may come with some bad experiences and negative influences; God is a good God he's able to turn all of our bad days into good days.

And give us a better mind even after waking up with a bad mind, some days our mind do not want to behave.

And we think bad thoughts and do bad things.

Let us cast down bad imagination, because one day were going hath to pay and give account of everything we do and say throughout the day, one day were going hath to pay for the deeds done in this body that God has giving us.

One day were going hath to give account of every bad word that comes out of our mouths from day to day without a doubt except we repent for all our wrong doings that was not right and done in God eyesight.

Many of things we done he was not please with; his spirit was filled with grievances from our own disobedient.

Pay day is coming, on that day the angels will be flying and people will be dying everyone will receive a check of the payment due unto them.

Payments will be made on time and everyone will receive their full amount of payment due unto them.

No deductions will taking out you will be giving everything you got coming, you will be paid in full, no negotiations will be made we will be paid in full for walking upright and all we endured along the way from day to day.

Pay day is coming hold on keep running for Jesus at the end you will get your reward.

A Crown of righteousness will be giving to those who uphold the truth of God word and strive to walk upright."

2Timothy 4:8 says *"Henceforth there is laid up for me a crown of righteousness, which the Lord the righteousness judge shall give me at that day; and not to me only but unto all them that love his appearing."* Amen.

And for all those who live a good life through trials and tribulations you stayed focus and kept pressing toward the mark of the high calling of Christ Jesus.

And you shall receive the crown of life, pay day is coming and we will be paid according to the works we done for God and the son man.

If we choose to be disobedient and rebellious to God word; and make our bed in hell and continue to play with the devil, abandon God stooping down to the devil level then that's where we will lay our head.

God is still just; pay day is coming you will be paid in full with the rewards of hell fire let us not make our bed in hell may our desirer be to come up higher and compel our minds on the most high God the father who looks down low, and sees all of our wrongs looking past our faults and seeing our needs and forgiving us for our sins, so we may have a chance to get right and make it into the kingdom of Heaven.

And dwell far beyond the sky, we must make up in our mind and choose this day who we are going to serve before we die.

Because once we take that ride over on the other side there is no turning back, and changing your mind in the middle of the ride.

We are going hath to live with and deal with the choices we make.

Once we leave out of here from this world it's too late to trying strait up our bed and lay our head in a different place of destination.

We are going hath to lay in the same bed we mess up on the same old dirty sheets that many never took timeout to wash them clean, let us clean up the sheets of our minds and wash our hearts by let God renew our minds.

Psalm 139 reads *"O Lord, thou hast search me, and known me. Thou knows my down sitting and mine uprising, thou understands my thoughts a far off. Thou compass my path and my lying down. And art acquainted with all my ways."*

Verse 4, *"For there is not a word in my mouth but lo, O Lord thou knows it all together. Thou hast set me behind and before and hast laid thou hand upon me. Such knowledge is too wonderful for me it is high I cannot attain unto it. Whiter shall I go from thy spirit or whiter shall I flee from thy present."*

Verse 8, *"If I ascend up into Heaven, thou art there; if I make my bed in hell, behold thou art there."*

God is an awesome God whom got all power in his hands.

He's everywhere all at the same time he's with you and me at the same time, he's with them up the street and those around the corner all at the same time.

He's in my house and your house at the same time; he's in the jail house, the court house, white house, and the hospitals all at the same time.

God is a good God and pay day is coming, may the works you do satisfy God keeping working for God it will pay off for you after awhile.

Pay day coming soon many of people will not be happy with the pay they will receive, many will be surprised of the amount of payment they will receive.

And many will be happy on that great day, everyone will be getting paid a lump sum for all the work they done.

Some will receive back pay, and holler-day pay the majority of them receiving holler-day pay are them who works for Satan day after day, it's going to be a whole lot of people laying on their backs paying for the wrongs they done, and a day of whole lot of hollering and screaming paid to them who did not repent.

It will also be a pay day bonuses given to those who work hard for the Lord and those who are sold out and gave him they all, living to bring glory unto him who gave his life for us, so that we may live.

Many standing in line to follow Jesus will be jumping for joy, singing and shouting because pay day has came they receive their rewards, and is about to enter into Heaven and spend the rest of they days with the lord.

And live in paradise, Many will be left behind sent to the lake of fire living in hell.

1Thessalonians 1:9 read *"Who shall be punish with everlasting destruction from the presence of the Lord and from the glory of his power."*

Matthew 7:22-23, *"I say unto you that many shall say unto me in that day Lord, Lord, have we not prophesied in thy name and in thy name have cast out devils and in thy name done many wonderful works."*

Matt 7: 11-12 says *"And then I will profess unto them I never knew you; depart from me ye worker of iniquity. I say unto you that many shall come from the east and the west, and shall sit down with Abraham, Isaac, and Jacob, in the kingdom of heaven."*

Verse 12, *"But the children of the kingdom shall be cast out into the outer darkness; there shall be weeping and gnashing of teeth."*

Pay day is coming and were going hath to pay for the wrongs we done that were displeasing unto God except we repent and turn from our wicket ways Amen.

May God bless you, and may the pay you receive from the Lord be the type of pay that makes you happy and say thank you lord.

You're Messenger Jimmy J.

Chapter Thirty-Five

Turn or Burn

Life is full of twist and turns: The road were traveling on is constantly turning taking us this way and that way leading us down the road of destruction, twisting around to an uphill struggle: that leads us to dark places sometimes we get lost constantly going around in circles. wasting energy and time burning up fuel that could have been used to pick somebody else up that may be lost and show them the way that leads to life; but first let us get our direction together; so that we can stop letting the devil lead us to twist our minds and turn us around.

Thought for Today: Those who use their Bible as a guide will never lose their sense of direction.

Read scripture: "2 Chronicles 7:14-16, 4-17.

Praise the Lord! Let us give praises to the most high, the one and only true God almighty.

He deserves all the honor and glory, and all the praises that are due to him because He is worthy. I come to share a word of encouragement and a little enlightenment on everyday practical living.

First and foremost we should be thankful for things being as well as they are, because they could be a whole lot worse.

We should be grateful to be in the land of the living because we could have been dead and gone but God being the God He is let us live on; so with that in mind, it should make us thankful and grateful to be alive, because there are so many people dying, young and old, dying from senseless killings, some commit suicide, yes some even take their own lives, and some are dying from sickness and disease and the list of the dead goes on.

Thank God our name is not found on the list of the dead, instead our name shall be found in the book of life.

We can be thankful for Jesus keeping us; let us be thankful that there is no tag found on our toe.

When you go to bed and look down at your feet if no tag can be found on your feet you ought to look up and say thank you Jesus.

It behooves me to tell you that tomorrow is not promised to us we ought to choose this day in which we shall serve.

God said in His word that we cannot serve two masters God and Mammon.

We shouldn't try to serve God and the devil, God is a just God so He left it to us to make a choice to become servants to God or a servant of the devil, if we be a servant of righteousness then we should live a life that's pleasing to Him, in order to please God we must love one another in spite of their imperfections we must help each other, we are to be humble, we must be faithful, and mindful of others.

God has the spirit of love and if we are children of God then we should walk in the likeness of Him and you shall live a good life turn from your wicked ways and be saved and learn of His ways.

Be not envious of evil workers who doth all manner of things.

Satan comes to steal your joy, kill your spirit and destroy your life.

But Jesus comes that you might have life; Satan is a deceiver, he likes to play deadly games that seem like fun, which when you are in darkness it may be fun, but if you play with the devil you are bound to get burned.

Do not play with the devil.

I repeat Do not play with the devil because sooner or later he will trick you out of your life, Satan is forever telling you to do the wrong thing and make it seem like it is ok to sin keeping you confused and always wanting you to lose, but as long as you keep your hand in the master's hand.

He can never defeat God's plan, and you will never lose. The devil lives in hell and dwells on earth to destroy peoples' lives; laughing at them when they cry and rejoicing when they die. He loves to hate and always looking for new roommates.

The last time I check the price it cost to stay in a hot hell hole was way too much, I couldn't afford it that price is out of my price range.

I have to find me a better place to stay.

There is a better place it is a place that doesn't cost as much; but provides much more, it is a place full of love, peace, joy and happiness.

It is a place where you don't have to pay to stay and the light and gas are free because there is no need for man made light, nor sunlight, because the landlord of this place name is Jesus and the sight of Jesus will shine so bright it will light up the whole entire place; and the fire from the souls of the saints and the warmth of His love will keep you from getting cold.

Save your life, your mind, body, and soul.

All you have to do is apply yourself and strive to live right and sign on the . . . dotted line, saying Lord forgive me and cleanse me from all my sin, then sign on the . . . dotted line again, saying I surrender meaning that you are turning it all over to Jesus.

Turn or Burn. Don't wait until the hearse brings you to the church and until things get worse.

Instead make your move first; put down the drugs and alcohol and anything else that may have you bound before they put you down permanently and repent for all of your sins. *Turn or burn:*

Turn away from evil thinking.

Turn away from perverse speaking.

Turn away from lying and cheating.

Turn your mind from that old way of thinking.

Turn to God and be blessed and say good-bye to that old mess. And hello to God and walk in the newness of life.

Be more like Christ.

Turn from doing evil, and live a life that is heaven bound not hell bound.

Turn to God or burn for the devil.

Turn or burn. If you turn to God and learn of His ways you will be blessed through knowledge you will attain and when you use the knowledge he puts in your brain you will see the blessings and the benefits of learning to be Christ like and just how beneficial his teachings can be to your life.

May you turn your life over to Jesus, He will bless you and continue to protect you and keep you from getting burned.

Turn to Jesus and learn; and He'll turn to you with open arms and forgiveness, He'll love you, bless you, and protect you out of compassion and concern.

I'm glad I passed up that hot hell hole and found me a better place to stay.

I'm on the waiting list to get into that great place; that place I found is way up yonder and is free to all who apply, but not all applications will be accepted they must first be checked by Jesus and come back clean with his stamp of approval then we are accepted and can make it in.

All mistakes and wrong doing that cause us to fall must be erased.

2Timothy 2:15 says "Study to show thyself approved unto God, a workman that needeth not to be ashamed, rightly dividing the word of truth.

May we study God's word and also study our own self; so that we may correct our wrongs into right everyday is a test and we are to study getting it wrong.

2 Timothy 2:16 says ***"But shun profane and vain babblings for they will increase to more ungodliness."***

In other words avoid that type of language. Turn away from and turn to some more uplifting words that will help you to grow more spiritual, rather than to stunt your growth, become a more positive person; who is striving to live right and talk right.

Be careful of the things you say and watchful of the games people play. There are a lot of games players out here because Satan has a lot of team players and remember he likes to play deadly games.

Some rough and hard to beat some smooth, but always wanting you to lose and stay confused, but just so you know God has already won that battle a long time ago.

Victory is yours and no weapon formed against you shall prosper.

We as children of God can conquer those things and people who come to conquer us.

Because he said in His word we are more than a conqueror.

We can overcome those things that come to bring us down.

Long as we have king Jesus on our side the enemy won't be able to defeat us. May we keep Jesus on the inside of the doors of our heart and not on the outside trying to get in.

Revelation 3:20-22 Reads *"Behold I stand at the door and knock: if any man hear my voice and open the door, I will come in to Him, and he with me."*

Many of people hear the voice of the lord knocking on the doors of their heart but refuse to answer and let him into their heart, and put down all those things that Satan uses to overtake their mind and make them fail to prevail in Christ. To him that overcomes will I grant to sit with me at my throne, even as I also overcame and am set down with my father in his throne."

Romans 12:21 says *"Be not overcome of evil, but overcome evil with good."*

We can overcome many things in our life simply by doing good and striving to walk upright verse 22 reads *"He that hath an ear let him hear what the spirit saith unto the churches."*

The spirit is saying turn or burn unto the people in the church today; because tomorrow is not promised.

Hope something was said to you has helped you turn closer to Jesus and walk upright.

May God bless you.

Your Messenger Jimmy J.

Chapter Thirty-Six

Stolen Jewels Seize And Kept For Evidence

Praise the lord, who is worthy to be praise and worth more than all the gold in the world.

Precious is the Lord Jesus Christ whom worked very hard seeking to save those which were lost. Precious is the lord who walked upright. Precious is the Lord who healed the sick and gave sight to the blind.

Precious is the Lord who open up blinded eyes and regulated confused minds, precious is the love of God.

John 3:16 says *"For God so loved the world that He gave his only begotten son, that whosoever believeth in him shall should not perish, but have everlasting life."*

Verse 17 *"For God sent not his son into the world to condemn the world but the world through him might the world be saved."*

Precious are the thoughts of Jesus who thought enough about us to call us friends, and also said he will never leave us nor forsake us; but he will always be with us even unto the end.

Precious is he who laid down his life for a friend and the sins of the world.

Precious is the blood of Jesus that gives life unto all men and women, precious is the day we accepted Jesus in our hearts.

We the people of God are precious Jewels stolen and kept for evidence.

Priceless Jewels on display being sold and stole many of God people who are precious Jewels are selling they self short, and many of our hearts and minds are being stole.

The day we accepted Jesus in our hearts was the day we became one of his precious Jewels.

We the children of God and people of the world are very precious in the sight of God we are very valuable like precious Jewels no piece of jewelry on earth can compare to a man, woman, boy, or girl, and what their worth in the sight of God.

We are a very valuable asset to the Kingdom of God.

Jesus Christ the king of kings whom posses all things is rich in houses and land, He's rich in love and rich in mercy, He's richly involved in the saving business.

He invested his life in me and you who have now became his precious Jewels, we are one of his most prize possession. Who he uses to bring him glory, and shine as a light on those living in darkness.

The Lord Jesus is a keeper of his most prize possessions.

He keeps all of his Jewels safe Constantly polishing them up keeping them shining looking like new putting them in a showcase on display for the world to see how the Lord Jesus take cares of his Jewels which is me and you.

He watches over us day and night, keeping his Jewels protected and in safe keeping for his self.

Many of his Jewels are clearly seen cleaned and renewed on display for the master use.

May you let God use you renew your minds and cleanse your hearts, so you may be used for the building of his kingdom.

There were times in our life when we let the devil use us to destroy ourselves and others.

Why not let God use you to help build up those who are broken and hurting through your life and the strength and love that he has gave unto you, restore broken lives walk upright and shine as precious Jewels spreading the good news.

Before we became precious Jewels of our Lord Jesus Christ many of our lives were like a heap of black coil hard and dirty with many rough edges and layers of crust.

But thanks be to God and the son of man who saw us laying under piles of dirt picked us up chip away all the crust, cleaned off all the dirt smooth out all the rough edges put us through the fire and burned off out all the filth from within us refined that heap of coal reshaped it renewed it mold it into a very valuable Jewels.

God is able to renew your minds and refine the way you think and live and mold you into a child of God from being a child of the devil.

St. John 3:20 read *"For everyone that doth evil hated the light, lest his deeds should be reproved."*

Verse 21 reads *"But he that doeth truth cometh to the light that his deeds may be made manifest, that they are wrought in God."*

Precious Jewels seize and kept for evidence sealed lock in a safe.

When you become lock into God your safe in the arms of Jesus.

Sealed and secure have no fear the Jewels that were stolen shall be returned back unto its rightful owner our father God the maker and creator of precious Jewels.

We as precious Jewels need to guard our hearts and lay hold of our minds feed our faith keep our trust and hope in the lord because we're living in a bad time surrounded with people with bad minds, even though times our bad and times our hard let us not make it easy for the devil to steal our joy; nor should we let him steal the Jewels of Jesus which are the saints of God.

Thieves and robbers are out to steal and kill for precious Jewels, be watchful and stay prayful.

St. John 10:10 *say "Verily verily, I say unto you he that enter not By the door into the sheepfold, but climbeth up some other way, the same is a thief and a robber."*

Jesus is the door He's the only way to heaven he's the mediator between us and God, he's the communicator to the Father in Heaven.

He's our vindicator and mind regulator He's our Salvation and protection.

He's our Lord and Savior that saved us and gave us a better mind and a second chance to get it right there's no other way we can make it in except we come through the door.

Jesus is the door walk toward the door there's room for the sick they will be made well there will be no more sickness once you enter the door of Jesus where he sits at the right hand of my Father God Almighty.

There's room for the poor they will be made rich precious Jewels returned back unto its rightful owner.

There be plenty of room for the righteous and many of those who are struggling trying to walk upright there be room for all who are lost trying to find they way, and have repented of their sin. One day God is going to bring this world to an end and the struggles will be all over.

There be room for thieves and robber who have repented of their wrongs and ask for forgiveness they will be given a new life and more than they could imagine, they want hath to steal no more or take what's your.

There's still room on the other side of the door for you and me and all those who are lost and have repented of their sin.

Let God free your mind from being bound down to this and bound to that you'll have total freedom you want have to worry no more about this or that.

Freedom waits on the other side of the door, but we must first repent and come to the door with a sincere heart. We can also be free here and now on this side of the door.

Keep knocking on the door of Jesus Matthew 7:7-8 says **"Asks and it shall be given you. For everyone that asked** *received; and he the seeketh findeth and to him that knocked it shall be open."*

The lord Jesus Christ is also knocking on the doors of our hearts today.

He said in his word if we would open the doors of our hearts He would come in and sup with us, He'll bring the food you need and eat of the table of God with you.

He will gives you the strength you need to make you strong and keep you standing when Satan trips you up, looking to see you fall.

God will help you stand. Rev3:18-20 reads *"I counsel thee to buy of me gold tried in the fire that thou mayest be rich; and white raiment, that thou mayest be clothed, and that the shame of thy, nakedness do not appear; and anoint thine eyes with eye salve that thou mayest see."*

Verse 19 *"As many as I love I rebuke and chasten; be zealous therefore and repent."* When we repent for our wrongs that we done and stay with God, it keeps us safe in the arms of Jesus and also keeps the devil from stealing the Jewels of the Lord Jesus Christ.

We the children of God are the precious Jewels Satan want to steal from God.

Verse 20 reads *"Behold I stand at the door and knock; if any man will hear my voice and open the door I will come in and sup with him and he with me."*

Praise the Lord let us be watchful and pray; may we guard the doors of our hearts because the devil will come like a thief in the night to steal away the Jewels of Jesus that he has put on display for the master use.

Such as people like you and myself to be sold to the kingdom of Satan where we would work for him day after day I must let it be known we were made for the master use brought with the precious blood of Jesus Christ.

Seize and took in possession by the hands of the Lord.

Thank God for Jesus who seized the stolen Jewels stop the devil in his tracks took back all the precious Jewels that the thief came to steal.

The thief comes to steal away your hearts and mind all the Jewels he can find.

He comes to steal away your spirit, body, and soul.

Let him that stole steal no more; for the Kingdom of heaven is yours.

Let us not be sold into slavery brought for half the price were worth sold into the kingdom of Satan, let us not sell our souls to the devil at no price offered because he will promise you the world and give you nothing but pain and misery grief and defeat. Stay with Jesus who paid for you in full the faithful one, who keeps his promise and will give you everything He promise you

2 Peter 1:3-4 reads *"According as his divine power hath giving unto us all things that pertain unto life and Godliness, through the kingdom of him that call us to glory and virtue. Whereby are giving unto us exceeding great and precious promise; that by these ye might*

be partaker of the divine nature, having escaped the corruption that is in the world through lust."

Thank you Jesus for seizing, and saving the stolen Jewels and returning them back to their owner God almighty may God bless you and keep you, Amen.

You're Messenger Jimmy J.

Capernaum_Synagogue

Chapter Thirty-Seven

He already knows and has already fixed it

God knows best. He knows what best for me, and he knows what best you, he knows what best for all of us.

He knows how to keep us safe and out of harms ways; he knows how to bless us when we stand in need of a blessing.

He knows how to heal us when we need a healing he knows how to regulate a confused fused mind, when our mind get con fused he knows how to straighten it out, when our hearts get heavy he knows how to ease the burden.

When we fall short in our Christian walk he knows how to pick us up, and put us back on track with a fresh anointing.

He knows how to get the dirt out of your heart and make it clean he even knows how to take out that old bad heart and give you a new heart in good working condition in satisfactory unto him who place it there.

May we satisfy God with the love in our hearts by sharing it with others who might not have any love in their hearts.

Psalm 145:17-21 reads *"The lord is righteous in all his ways, and holy in all his work, the lord is nigh to all them that call on him."*

He will fulfill the desires of them that fear him; he will also hear they cry and will save them.

He heard the cry's of all his people and he will come and see about you.

The lord preserveth all them that love him but ALL the wicket will he destroy.

Verse 21 *"My mouth shall speak the praise of the lord; and let all flesh bless his holy name forever and ever."*

Thanks be to God who save us and preserved us.

Even when we were in out there in our wrong doings doing all kinds of wrong doings.

He watches over us and saved us until this present day.

And is still watching over us preserving us for a later date, giving us time to get it right.

May we die to the sin in our lives and be more obedient to God word, be a blessing to someone else that less fortunate than yourself, God said in his word for what you do unto the least one of my children you do the same unto me.

God knew us before we were form in our mother's womb.

He knows us all from head to toe, he watch us grow and he knows all about us, He knows when were up and he knows when were down, He knows when were off track and have allowed our sins to set us back.

He knows when were on point fighting on the front line for righteousness to abide in our life.

He seen the many bad seeds we sowed and he seen the good as well, he applaud us for our good success, He have also seen us fail as we trying to walk upright for him.

He's not happy with all of our mess of constantly sinning, he died for us to give us life, thank God for Jesus the scriptures tells me he died but he got up 3 days later and rose with all power; and ascended on high where he now sits at the right hand of the Father in Heaven.

He got up with all power in his hands, he's rich in mercy his word tells me that his mercy is renewed every morning he sits high on the throne sees all of our wrongs.

He knows all of our addresses and where we are at in our Christian walk.

There is nothing we can do are say that he does not already know.

H e already knows what in our mind and hearts; he already knows that you're weak.

And the devil comes to swift you as wheat and leaves you lifeless.
M any of us are bound to this and bound to that, but he knows about everything were going through many of our heads are hanging low and our minds are confused.

Jesus is the only one who is able to free you from been bound down and regulate that confused mind.

HE already knows were going to hath called on him, he already knows he going hath to come to our rescue and pick us up, he already know he is going hath lift up a bowed down head.

He already know about fornication and adultery in the church and out of the church he already know about our evil thoughts and lustful desires he already know about homosexuality and lesbians in various churches and out in the world.

He already know about all the back sliders slipping and dipping into sin, he already know about all false pretender and under handed preachers deceiving themselves and God peoples.

Who use God ministry deceitful and for self gain God shall rain on just and the unjust.

He knows who will follow him and he know those who will follow after Satan, and he know those who will stand on that sure foundation of Jesus Christ, and those who will up hold the truth of God Word.

He knows the true worshipper who will worship him in spirit and truth.
He knows those who are playing, and he knows those who are sincere.

He also knows how to fix anything or anyone that may be broken.

If your heart is broken God is able to fix it for you and put it back together again.

If your life broken God is able to restore broken lives and make you whole through his word; continue to read his word, his word will save your soul.

God will fix it for you reason I know because he fix it for me one day when he saved my life that was the day Satan tried to take my life, but God said no devil you cannot have him.

He belongs to me, he fixed for me and let me live that was a day I will never forget that day of 2-26-89 I got shot in the back of head left on the side of the road for dead.

That devil came close to stealing my life death was nearby starring me in the face I call on Jesus he heard my cry came closer to me shower me with his love moved that devil out of the way saved me with his grace and mercy he is the reason why I still live today.

He came to my rescue and saved me and did what he said he would do.

He said in his word I'll never leave you or forsake you.

He fixed me. He fixed for my mother when He delivered her from cancer 8 years ago she is still cancer free in the land of the living doing find serving the Lord and taking care of her husband and telling others about the goodness of the lord he also knew he was going to hath to fix it for my brother Pastor Earl Jordan who appeared to be a failure failing to have success over drugs and alcohol once again Jesus fixed it for my brother Earl and gave him power to overcome drugs and alcohol Jesus fixed for him and gave him great success to become a minister.

And from a minister he became a pastor of his own church called Crusade for Christ Christian Ministry Church.

He did it for us and he'll do it you.

He'll fix's whatever broken no matter how bad the situation may seen turn it over to Jesus he can fix any and everything you do not have to beg or pay him he said in his word just ask in faith and believe and He will do it for you freely.

Psalm 146-1-8 reads *"Praise ye the Lord praise the lord oh my soul."*

Verse 2 *"While I live I sing praise unto my God while I have any being."*

Verse 3 reads *"Put not your trust in Princes. Nor in the son of man whom there is no help."*

Verse 4, read *"His breath go forth he returned to his earth in that very day and his thoughts perish."*

Verse 5 *"Happy is he that hath the God of Jacob for his help, whose hope is in the lord his God."*

Verse 6 *"Which made heaven and earth, and the sea and all that there in."*

Verse 7 *"Which executed judgment for the oppressed; which give'th food to the hungry."*

Verse 8 *"The Lord openeth the eyes of the blind; the lord raised them that are bowed down; the lord loveth the righteous he will fix it for those he love and for those who love him."*

Jesus has much love for the world; and many people of the world today love him, he fixed it for the whole world one day when he went to the cross at Calvary.

Luke 9:22 says *"The son of man must suffer many things and be rejected of the elders and chief priests and scribes and be slain and be raised on the third day."*

Luke 9:23 says *"And to them all, if any man will come after me let him deny himself take up his cross daily and follow me"*

Let us take up the cross in our life which is those things that keeps us bound constantly causing us to sin.

But thanks be to God for sending his son into the world to die for our sins

He came to set the captive free he set the whole world free when he died on the cross at Calvary. He went to the cross caring us on his mind, He went to the cross for us who were blind He went to the cross for all who were lost.

He went to the cross carrying a heavy load of sin, he took on sins of the world HE went to the cross willfully.

He went to the cross with his mind made up.

He already knew what he was going to do for me and you.

He went to the cross at Calvary bravery he had no fear; everyone who came against him to beat him hurt him reputably, and talk about him, he said forgive them father for they know not what they do.

He went to the cross in agony, suffering for you and me he went to the cross to cross tired and barely able to walk he went to cross hurting and bruising; He went to the cross and died at Calvary for the lost.

Isaiah 53:4-5 says *"Surely he hast borne our grief's and carry our sorrows; yet we did esteem him stricken; smitten of God and afflicted. But he was wounded for our transgressions bruise for our iniquities the chastisement of our peace was upon him."*

He already knew and he had already fix it for you, hoping something was said to let you know he cares and is willing and able to fix it for you, May God Bless you and keep you.

Your Messenger Jimmy J.

Chapter Thirty-Eight

There is strength in repentance

Trouble doesn't last always, but we must repent of our sins and wrong doings, and ask God for forgiveness; move on and do better.

Keep striving, climbing to go higher and higher, growing stronger and stronger in the Lord.

Own up to your faults and failures, confess to God repent and represent the Holy sent one Amen.

Psalm 34:14-15

"Depart from evil, and do good; seek peace and pursue it

The eyes of the Lord are upon the righteous, and his ears are open unto their cry."

There is strength in repentance, we all have been down in the valley and walked in the shadow of death.

We all have set in the seat of despair sin have flared up in all our life. We all have step in a moment of weakness.

We all have had a appetite for the temptations of life, we all laid in sin and slept in the lust of our minds. God is an on time God He heard the cries of his people crying out for help, he will dry the eyes of those who are weeping from sorrows grief mystery and pain.

Of hurting lost people, he said in his word come unto me all those who are heavy laden and I will give you rest. If your burdened down give it to the Lord.

He said in his word my yoke easy and my burden is light He might not come when you want him to but when he come He will be right on time, Amen sometime we hath to bow to our knees in repentance and repent for the things we done that were wrong and displeasing in God eye sight. Sometimes we hath to say look Lord I Know I been wrong I'm sorry for my wrong doings, look in on me and strengthen me in the area's where I am weak, when I am weak Lord you are strong. But when you look my way and strengthen me then I become strong. There is strength in repentance and a Godly sorrow touches the heart of God. He moves quickly to rescue a broken and contrite heart.

When your down in sorrow's valley God will pick you up and bring you over into the land of happiness he will free your mind from thinking about circumstances and situations that you cannot do anything about.

Put all of trust and faith in God and the son of man over in His hands.

Repentance frees you up from being bound down.

Repentance puts you right standards with God. Sometimes we to say Lord I know I been wrong, but if I haven't been too wrong forgive me of my sins and cleanse my heart.

He said in his word ask and it shall be giving thee, seek and ye shall find, knock and the door will be open.

Lets us call on God; ask for what you want, and the things you stand in needs of.

If you want joy ask the Lord to come into your life and give you joy.

If you stand in need of repentance ask to be forgiving and repent mean it from your heart.

He will clean you up and give you a brand new start; he will pick up and carry you to a higher level in your Christian walk.

Let go and let God, sometimes we hath to let go things and people that are a hinder to us and our growth in Christ as we strive to do better and grow closer and be more like Christ.

Let go hatred, envy and strife, let go kayos and confusion, let go of sin, he will be a fence of protection all around us.

He's our bridge over trouble waters, He's our way maker, He's our way out of trouble and confusion, He is our bread when we are hungry and water when we are thirsty.

He's our vindicator and protector, He's a keeper and a mind regulator, and He's the answer to all of our problems.

He's our all and all he's the one who will pick you up when you fall.

There's strength in repentance there's strength and power in the love God.

You give strength to others when you represent the Holy sent one, the one and only King of Kings, the Lord Jehovah Javier my provider, that bright morning star that shines light on darkness the prince of peace who gave you peace in the mind and places where confusion use to be.

He's able to create a clean heart in you; he's able to give you good mind even after waking up with bad mind.

He's able to calm the storms in your life; He's able to stand you up after the devil has beaten you down.

Repent and represent the one who died for you He represented the love of his father God almighty, and his love for the world which included you and me.

Acts 8:22 says *"Repent therefore of this thy wickedness, and pray God if perhaps the thoughts of thine heart may be forgiven."*

Verse 23 reads *"For I perceive that the gall of bitterness and in the bond of iniquity."*

Many of us are still bound with iniquities and need to repent be set free and strengthen to walk upright, and represent my friend who laid down his life for his friends, and said He will be with us all ways even unto the end.

He said in his word he will never leave us nor forsake us. Matt 3:2 reads *"In those days came John the Baptist preaching in the wilderness of Judea's and saying repent ye for the Kingdom of Heaven is at hand."*

Verse 3 reads *"For this is he that was spoken of by the prophet Eas-ias, saying the voice of one crying in the wilderness, prepare ye the way of the Lord, make his path straight."*

Many preachers are still preaching that same word today in these days in the City County Suburban areas and churches all across the world.

Saying repent ye for the Kingdom of Heaven is at hand, many of us today are crying in the wildness and need to repent and prepare ye the way of the Lord make his path straight.

The path that leads into the Kingdom of Heaven is the road of righteous. Known as the straight and narrow path.

If your traveling on the broad road doing everything under the sun, running with Satan hating to do what's right building your home on the road of destruction constantly making wrong turns getting set back making it hard to get to your destinations.

We must come to a stop from going down the wrong road wasting time constantly being turn around switch avenues and get on the right road, head down the road of righteousness you will see better view and a new you there is strength in repentance.

Luke 13:3 reads *"I tell you nay; but except ye repent ye shall likewise perish."* Jesus was speaking concerning the Gal-i-lae'-ans, these Gal-i-lae-ans were sinner above all gal-ians."

This same word of repentance goes' for us today of all race and nationally except we repent ye shall all likewise perish die in your sins.

Thank God for his love and mercy who gives us grace and renews his mercy every morning allowing us time and time again to repent and get right with God.

Luke 15:7 says *"I say unto you that likewise joy shall be in Heaven over one sinner that repented more than over ninety and nine just person which needed no repentance."*

We all have done something that we need to repent for, let us repent and get right with God, according to this word the angel in Heaven will be rejoicing over that sinner man, women, boy, or girl.

There strength in repentance, repentance put you in right standard with the one who forgives for all of your sins.

As long as the blood still runs warm in your veins you still have a chance to change.

You're Messenger Jimmy J.

Chapter Thirty-Nine

Looking through the eyes of Jesus

Praise the Lord Thank God for Jesus who look unto his Father and saw fit to give himself to save a lost and dying world Amen.

May we take a look at ourselves through the eyes of Jesus, and you will see a wretched man or women undone, far from been right in God eye sight. Take a look at yourselves through the eyes of Jesus and you will see how short you are from lining up with his word. Take a look inside yourselves and see what you're made of; you will find out that you are made of the spirit of God. The everlasting God almighty creator of the world, he's the one who made you form you in your mother womb before you were ever born. Amen he gave us life twice, and we are going hath to die twice before we make it in to heaven. Were going hath to die the physical death, and were going hath to die to the sin within us Amen. Thank God for Jesus who gave us a mouth to talk with may we talk of his goodness, thank God for Jesus who gave us life and legs to walk with may we walk worthy and continue to strive to walk upright, he put breath in our bodies, may we live for him. He gave us eyes to see with, May we see ourselves and other the way Jesus sees us, may we look through the eyes of Jesus and zero in on our wrong doings, faults and failures, and see about correcting our wrongs into rights successfully do our best. Let us look through the eyes of Jesus and see the power that is inside of you. May you see how strong you really are? Philippians 4; 13 say ***"I can do all things through Christ which strengthen me."*** So with that in mind let us not be so quick to bend the truth and continue in sin. May we continue to strive to win the prize of Jesus? May we look and see the victory that's already been won by the one and only the son of man better known as Jesus Christ who rules supreme. Take a look at yourselves through the eyes of Jesus and see how bless you are. Take a look at yourselves though the eyes of Jesus and see how far you're off, and that you need his help, because we cannot make it without him. But with him we can do many of things and make our life a success because truly we are blessed.

Psalm 33:18-22 reads ***"Behold, the eyes of the Lord is upon them that fear him, upon them that hope in his mercy; to deliver their souls from death and keep them alive in famine. Our soul waited for the lord; he is our help and shield. For our heart shall rejoice in him, because we have trusted in his holy name. let thy mercy o Lord be upon us, according as we hope in thee."***

May we put our hope in the Lord and more trust in his word, so that he may continue to give us more mercy. 2Corinthian 2:9 "But as it is written, eyes have not seen, nor ears heard, neither have enter into the hearts of man the things which God hath prepared and in stored for those who love him."

Hold on to what right keep showing love toward God and others good things will be rewarded unto you. Continue to look through the eyes of Jesus for then our way won't be so dark and cloudy days will be much brighter. When you look through the eyes of Jesus it will help you see better, clearer, and in pure form, looking through the eyes of Jesus also helps you to see danger before it comes.

When you see other people, don't focus on their wrongs, look through the eyes of Jesus and see if you can help them by saying something that may lead them to Christ, So when they look at you they will see the good in you and not focus on your wrongs and bad behavior. Instead they will see and know that you stand for the righteous of God Amen. When you see other people acting bad being rude displaying a negative attitude, don't put thumbs down on them, instead put your finger of love on them lift them up in prayer, and look at them through the eyes of Jesus when people do you wrong, mistreat you and put you down, talk about you and scandalize your name remain humble and remember they talk about Jesus Christ mistreated him, put him down scandalize his name and hung him up high leaving him to die. He endured much persecution, grief, misery and pain. But still remain humble, and endured the cross of crucifixion; we too must endure persecution, agony grief, misery and pain. And learn to bear our cross of suffering remain humble and faithful unto God because the thief comes steal your spirit, kill your joy, and destroy your life. Crucifying us daily leaving us hanging on empty promise, bound wrapped in sin caught up in this and caught up in that. But let us look at ourselves though the eyes of Jesus, then we will be able untangle ourselves from being wrapped up in sin caught up in this and caught up in that, when you look at yourselves though the eyes Jesus he show you how to untie the knot Satan has tied you into. He'll help you loosen the grip being tied up and bound down. Keep looking at yourselves and others through the eyes of Jesus and soon you will be free Amen. There too many people looking at their selves through the eyes of the devil keeping each other tied up and bound down constantly stooping unto the devil's level at the bottom floor of destruction, where we are not able to see know more than what he let us see. Nor can we go no further than the leash of Satan allows you to go. But when you come up higher to the top floor of your minds and let God renew your minds, then you become free and are no longer bound to this and that, then is when you will be able to see all the good things God has in stored for you. That Satan kept away from you by blinding your eyes to the gifts and promises of God. Because he has kept many of us blinded and bound down not letting you see what God has in stored for you. But when you look through the eyes of Jesus he opens up those blinded eyes.

And let you see that the world belongs to him and all that's therein. When you look at the world through the eyes of Jesus you'll be able to see the greatness of God, the power, his might and insight, that he place in our life through the sacrificing of his son Jesus Christ who died on the cross for our sins and rose from the grave site where they laid him. According to the scriptures 1Corinthian 15:3-4 reads ***"For I delivered unto you first of all that which I also received, how that Christ died for our sins."***

According to scriptures 1 Cor.e4 tells us that he was buried, and that he rose again the third day according to the scriptures may you receive the words Paul delivered unto us through the scriptures giving Amen. When Jesus rose on that third day, he rose with all power in his hands, he rose with love and kindness, knowledge beyond our understanding. Many could not understand the love of Jesus many still could not understand his love for the world. And many find it hard to understand and take heed to the words of knowledge they read that's being written and giving for exhortation and inspiration to the affecting of the saints and sinners. That something may be said that will affect them and inspire them to do better Amen.

1John 2:15-17 reads "Love not the world, neither the things that are in the world. If any man love the world the love of the father is not in him." Verse 16 "For all that is in the world, the lust of the flesh, the lust of the eyes, and the pride of life, is not of the Father, but is of the world.

Verse 17 says "And the world passeth away, away and the lust there of; but he that doe's the will of God abideth forever."

Let us continue to do the will of my father in heaven. Amen. As we live from day to day and go from place to place, look at people and places through the eyes of Jesus because looking through the lust of the eyes are only a rush to build a nest of sin. Bad thoughts going to come and go, but we do not have to let them stay and build a nest within us Amen. The lust of the eyes is a wide range of wanting and desiring to fulfill and satisfy the flesh. God do not take pride in our mess, but let us take pride in ourselves and not the things of this world. Let us be steadfast and take pride in abiding in God word. Look though the eyes of Jesus and walk in his footsteps, Amen.

You're Messenger Jimmy J.

HE CHANGED THE COURSE
OF
HISTORY
He was a man for our times,
Like Moses in his day,
For God used him mightily,
To pave a better way.
A way of peaceful existence,
Between blacks and whites,
And a greater degree of freedom,
With a respect for human rights.
Though it cost his life,
His death was not in vain
For he helped change the course
of history.

Chapter Forty

A Tribute to Dr. Martin Luther King Jr. It's a new day America

Praise the lord, thank God for Dr. Martin Luther King who came into the world at a bad and brutal time, but when he left this world, The world was in much better shape than it was before he came, when he was here justice begin to reign. Bad times still exist but it is not nearly the same: Take some time and give a piece of your mind to the encouraging and thoughtful words about a man who cared so much about humanity and equal rights for all.

May these words help you in some shape, form, or fashion to show love? And treat each others fair. The late great Dr. Martin Luther King Jr. Was a man who change the way we live our lives, he was a man who fought for us and taught us about our rights, he devoted his life to fight for civil rights and equal Justice for all. He was a man who had a dream, his dream included you and me and the rest of the world too.

The dream was so big that it reach heaven and touch God. He smile down on Dr. King and granted him everything that he was fight far. God heard the news that King went around preaching from city to city marching on his feet trying to change the mean streets of violence, God saw the abuse he was taken each day that he was awaken Dr. Martin Luther King continue to preach out his dream he was making great success in reaching the hearts and minds of the people everywhere but unfortunately everyone did not like what he was preaching: People started to threaten him and attack his family, life became very hard for this great man to live. So God called him home, but his dream still lives on up until this day. Thank the lord for fulfilling his dream and letting things be as well as they are. We are living in a new day in America, we are living in a new time, with new and modering things, such as talking cars and talking cell phones cell phones, computers, digital cameras, IPods, laptops deep fryers, watches, fancy stoves books made into movies and so much more. We have a lot to be thankful for in this day and time, because people we know that are dead and gone on to live with the lord did not have the things we have in our life time today.

Thank God for giving man wisdom and knowledge to the people of the world today to make all these things possible: And we thank God for Jesus as well as Dr. martin Luther King who gave us a new start in life by fighting for equal rights, here we are over 44 years later still living in that same dream that came to a man name Dr, Martin Luther King Jr.; his dream is still effective here in 2013 as it was back then in 1968 when he died fighting for equal rights. People all over the world is grateful for the things he done for the people in America and Nationwide through his speaking out on our people living in a unjust society. People all around the world are giving thanks and tributes to Dr. Martin King, for sharing his dream and trying to bring people of the world together.

He deserves to be honored, and celebrated for his life achievement, that's why this tribute is written to the great Dr. Martin Luther King Jr. He change the way of the world from people living in an unjust society to a livable and justifiable society. Thank God for Dr. Martin Luther King Jr. who pass by our way and change the mean evil streets of hatred and prejudice to having peace and harmony with one another. I just want to say thanks to Dr. Martin Luther King Jr. for sharing his dream with us and giving us hope to see a better day, and a greater tomorrow, thank him in your hearts for encouraging us and giving us belief in our times of sorrow and grief: He change hearts fill with hate to hearts of love, he change frown into smiles through his hard work of fighting for peace and justice for all. He change feeling of despire to feeling of hope and a feeling to live and not die, because he gave us freedom, we have freedom from been beat, because we refused to do a certain thing that someone else requires of us to do. We have freedom from been told to go sit at the back of the bus because you are black, we have freedom from been told to get up out of your seat on the bus if your black and let some white person sit down and have your seat. We have freedom from been told we can't eat at a white own restaurants, we have freedom from been told we can't book a room at a white own hotel or motel, we have freedom from been afraid to go to sleep at night because someone might throw a fire bomb through your window while you're sleeping and burn your house down. Back then our people were living in some very mean and evil days, and many of the people couldn't even imagine Justice been made for all humanity. This tribute is written for Dr. Martin Luther King birthday, and for birthing a new day in America. We are now able to sit and ride at the front of the bus, were now able to drive the bus, and some of us are now able to buy the bus and the bus station if so desired, we are now able to book a room at a white own hotels or motel, black people are now able to run the hotels or motels and buy them if so desired. We no longer hath to be afraid to go to sleep in our own homes Dr. Martin Luther King. Has made a way through fighting for Justice and equal rights, we can now at least sleep in peace. But let us thank God for the peace he gives us in our minds and hearts: with that Jesus peace within us gives us a better determination to strive and do better and keep moving up scale further and further. If you really take a look at the situation at hand and the people in your own neighborhood, its only about 2 or 3out of every 10 who are successfully and financially doing good, so you see the black man is still far from living the America dream, the black man is still not that far up scale and not that far from poverty, most of us are still living in poverty. Struggling and suffering, still living in a unjust society. Dr King made a big change for the better in our society, but we still have some injustice going on in every town, and state across the world. Maybe the only true justice that we will ever experience is the true justice from above; let justice that comes from above make the crooked places straight and the rough places smooth. God is a Just God and he is able to fix's all things and make them better for all of us. But its true Dr. Martin Luther King Jr. did birth a new day in America. But I must say we are living in some dangerous and perilous times, the days are still evil even though were living in a new day , we must continue to

God's Spoken Word In Plain View

pray for peace and Justice for all, we need peace in the middle east, and peace in our own homes, let peace rain on the unrighteous as well as the righteous, let peace rain everywhere that evil roams. Because we're still living in a time where evil and prejudice still floats in the air we breathe. But we the people of God must walk by faith, and not by sight, even though we see, hear, and feel these bad spirits, let us not look upon them and act on their level let us look upon God and act on the level he would have us to operate on, and live by his will, walking through our polluted streets of evil and hatred. Walking in love filled with peace and love from above.

May we continue to live out Kings Dream and display some of the same characteristics of faith in our daily lives?

May God bless you?

And may you continue to keep

The dream alive, your Messenger Jimmy J.

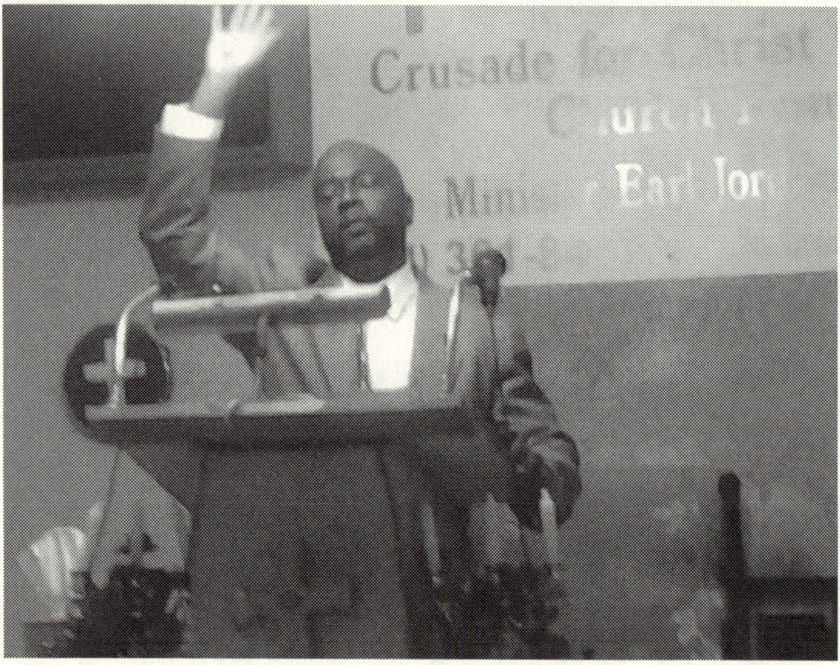
Crusade

Chapter Forty-One

Feet Shod With The Preparation Of The Gospel Peace

Praise the Lord saint's, praise him because he worthy, God is a good God, he deserves all the honor and praises due unto him; let us thank him for things being as well as they are, let us thank him for his son Jesus Christ who went around spreading the gospel. The gospel is a part of God's amour; please take heed to the word you read as I speak to your minds concerning having your feet shod with the preparation of the Gospel. To have our feet shod with the preparation of the gospel of peace means to be filled with God word, when your cover with God word he will protect you through your obedient to his word God word is the good news which we should use to prepare ourselves for the storms ahead Amen. We are to protect our hearts with God word the same way we protect our body with cloths, when we get fully dress the cloths keeps the body warm and protected from getting cold and sick in the winter time just like summer cloths keeps the body cool in the summer, and the shoes protects the feet at all times and gives you support that helps you walk better. The shoes protects the feet from getting wet in the rain, the shoes protects the feet from freezing in the snow. The shoes protect the feet from getting hurt from rock or glass. The same way the word of God can keep you and protect you from falling into sin getting hurt over and over again. The word of God can save you from destruction, and doing corruptible things.

Having your feet shod with the preparation of the gospel of peace will keep you walking upright and doing things that are right and pleasing in God eye sight. Having your feet shod with the gospel of peace, means that you should always be prepared to tell someone about the good news of God and how he sent his only begotten son Jesus Christ to die for the sins of this world. The good news is when Jesus died He left us a comforter whom is the Holy Spirit which will teach us all things and be with us always.

And the father in heaven left us his instruction on how to live right, the good news about the gospel is God left written instruction on the way we should live. All we hath to do is pick up the bible and read the gospel for ourselves and his word will teach you all you need to know. Having your feet shod with the preparation of the gospel of peace means to be prepared to go tell the world that Jesus Christ is alive and he is able to save your soul, having your feet shod means that you can go tell the world that Jesus is a healer, having your feet shod with the preparation of the gospel of peace means you can go tell the world Jesus is a deliver, having your feet shod with the gospel of peace, means that we must walk in love.

Having your feet shod with the gospel of peace means we must display meekness and kindness, It means that you have peace, and you will not be so easily to argue or fight. If you have the gospel you will have freedom from upsetting thoughts or feeling. It means to be humble, it means to be at harmony among the people, and spread the word of God with meekness, the gospel of peace means putting up with pain or troubles without complaints it means to be calm and have self control. Having your feet shod with the gospel of peace means one should have a peace of mind; it means one should have forgiveness in their heart, in spite of the wrongs someone do to you. Let the peace of Christ rule in your hearts since we as member of one body, we are called to peace. And let the word of Christ dwell in you richly as you teach and admonish one another with all wisdom as you sing songs hymns and spiritual songs with gratitude in your hearts to God, and whatever you do, whether in word or deed, do it all in the name of the Lord Jesus giving thanks to God the Father through him.

May we keep our affection on things above, may we love one another and strive for that Jesus peace, and then our hearts will be full of joy. May God bless you and forever keep your feet shod with the gospel of peace Amen.

Walk with Jesus follow in his footsteps and talk to him every step of the way, as you travel up the road of righteous may you look around for some lost soul waiting to be found, reach out your hand of love to them invite them to come along with you and tell them about King Jesus who sits high above at the right hand of his Father God Almighty who looks down low and sees all of our wrongs and knows exactly where we are at in Christian walk God sees all and he knows all, he knows we're going to see many side shows along the way, he knows were going to see many things to tempt us to fall into diver temptation, and he knows we are going to fall day to day. If and when we fall let us call on the one who is going to pick us up Amen. That someone is Jesus who will give us the strength we need to stand and go on let us strive to stay on the right road, keep walking with Jesus right or wrong, because Jesus is our help he is able to correct our wrongs into rights keep striving to walk upright so that your feet may continually be shod with the gospel of peace, keep talking to those lost souls that Satan holds in his hands let them know about God Almighty who holds the world in his hands and he is able to provide you with the things you need and want the God I serve is able to protect you and keep you safe, bless you heal you from any sickness and deliver you out of the troubles that Satan may bring your way from day to day, but as long as we have God on our side he more than the world against us, have no fear when Jesus is here and he's always nearby so let God use you to spread the good news Amen.

Your Messenger Jimmy J.

Chapter Forty-Two

Forever Being Taught and Never Learning

I heard it's been said fools perish from the lack of knowledge, many people who have died and left this world for foolish and sinful reason could have still been here today if they would have listen and took heed to the teaching been taught b y the inspiring knowledge of God giving to those who speak the word of God concerning his son Jesus Christ, God has sent many of his messenger to speak his word, but many of us have failed to listen and take heed to the word of God that has been spoken to us, and failed to let his word soak in us renew our minds and wash our hearts clean. Sacrifice is better than disobedient its better to give up those things we like doing that displeases God, rather than being disobedient unto God and doing things ungodly and unlike God. Let us not do those do those things that displeases God. We are forever been taught and never learning.

Psalm 13:1 *"Hear me when I call, O God of my righteousness; thou hast enlarge me when I was in distress; have mercy upon me and hear my prayer."*

Thought for today: Those who use their bible as a guild will never lose their sense of direction. When will we learn to live a life that's pleasing in God eye sight, and how can we learn to live, we must first be taught through the word of God. There's many ways one can learn from we can learn from each other, which means there will be many ways different ways that one can learn, one can learn from school how to read and write, and the basic fundamental of life, we can also learn from our mistake which is one of our best teacher, and the one that has the most impact on our life because our mistakes and failures tells us exactly where we went wrong at and lets us know what we need to do to fix's the situation our mistakes is able to make us sit down and listen. When will we learn, I heard many people say keep living you will learn many of things, because the world has a much to give both good and bad.

There have been much offered to us both good and bad, but most of us seems to cling to the bad things, rather than the good things of God. We know everything that comes our way is not going to be good for us nor will everyone be good to you. So we hath to take the good with the bad. Sometimes in life we hath to also learn to keep our mouths shut, and sometimes we also hath to learn to walk away from things, and sometimes we hath to run away from different situation, then there are times we must stand up and face our opponent head on and learn to live with and deal with our adversity as they come Amen. Many trails and tribulation going to come our way on the daily basic but we must learn to face them. And when we learn to live the right way that's when we learn to obey the word of God, God word. Will save your soul and make you whole. If you take heed to the teaching of Jesus that's when you begin to learn and grow into a mature Christian and has tasted the word, and have grown up and became strong in the knowledge of his word, you can now chew on the meat of his word to fill your minds with God spirit. Not only will you fill your minds with God spirit you will also be led by his spirit, he will also fill your hearts with love and strengthen your minds. Amen.

To help you think right and do right the milk of his word makes your bones strong so that can stand up and be able to stand against the test and trails that comes your way to rob you of your joy when tests and trails comes upon you, they come to make you strong that's the reason why you should count them all joy, because they will strengthen you for the journey ahead, when one possess real genuine faith it does not snap at the breaking point. That's the kind of faith we need to keep us and help us hold on until something or someone comes along and help us to do better, I found out that it don't take a whole lot of faith just a little bit is all you need and that little bit faith will take you a long way and move big mountains; Jesus said in his word if we have the faith as a grain of mustard seed ye can say unto this mountain, remove; and nothing shall be impossible unto you. Amen

God is able to remove the mountains of trouble in your life, He's able to remove confusion and the desire of living a negative and wrongful life and give you the desire of want to live a righteous life. Amen.

Because of your unbelief *"Verily I say unto you if you have faith as a grain of mustard seed you can say unto a mountain move and it shall be moved."* Now that's powerful we too can have that same power working in our life if we only believe in Jesus, if you just believe in him a little bit he will show you a whole lot through your faith and his works, and when he get through showing you his power and what he can do it will build up your faith and give you a stronger belief in him. So that you may come to believe in him and put your trust in him. O faithless generation how long shall we continue to live a life displeasing unto God and doubting in his word, not believing that through faith we can do all things, Jesus said himself if thou can believe all things are possible to him that believe. Some of us have little mountains and some of us have big mountains, and some of us have mountain in between, but all of them seems to be hard to climb and get on top of. Were forever being taught how to climb and overcome the mountains in our life but never learning how to chunk away the small pieces of that mountain bit by bit until you cut down the tree of troubles and mountain of despire.

We can look at mountains as obstacle, or problem or basically anything that hinder you from moving forward in your Christian walk or life period. Through faith in God and the power of prayer you shall be able to move any mountain big or small through your faith and trust in God you can remove them all. 1 Timothy 1:9 says ***"This is a faithful saying and worthy of all accept ion therefore we both labor and suffer reproach, because we trust in the living God who is the savior of all men especially those that believe in God and know he is able to do all things except fail."*** But how long will we continue on doing wrong, will we wait until we get a chance to ride in that long Hearse going to take you to a place where you won't return from and leave you laying in a dark empty spot is where your rides stop or will you make your move first while you still have a time to make up in your mind and learn to live a life that's pleasing in God eye sight. May you get it right before you hath to take that long sleep in the night, may you continue to live right and hold on to God word and hold on to it tight.

Satan has driven many of us to a dark empty spot in our minds and in our life, and is still driving many of us today taking us for a ride trying to get us to lay in that in that long hearse, blinding us from seeing our best, finding ourselves at our worst. We are forever being taught God's word and how to live right, but it seems like we the children of God and people of the world never learn to lean and depend on God. There are a whole lot of us who are quick to listen and adapt to the wrong thing, many of us are very smart in learning how to live the wrong way. And only a few of us who have learned two wrongs don't make a right. Some people still think that it's right to do other people wrong because others people have done you wrong. But Jesus said in his word do good unto the ones that do bad and evil things unto you, and despitefully use you and bless those who curse you Amen.

In order to learn we must first be taught then we study and concentrate on keeping our minds focus and consecrate our hearts and minds to the Lord, and receive his blessing and rewards. Many people of the world today are forever been taught to live a lie of the devil, we have too many people living negative lives' and lies of the devil, and not enough people learning to live the truth in Christ and walk up right before the Lord thy God.

Galatians 2:20 tell us how to live the truth in Christ says I *am crucified with Christ*. Nevertheless I live, yet not I but Christ lives in me; and the life which I now live in the flesh, I live by faith of God who died for us, may we crucify the sin in our life, and die daily to the sin within us for Christ. Amen."

Galatians 5:24-25 reads and they that are Christ's have crucified the flesh with affections and lust. V25: *"If we live in the spirit let us walk in the spirit."* Titus 2:11-12 tells us *"For the grace of God that bringeth salvation hath appeared to all men, that denying ungodliness and worldly lust, we should live soberly, righteously, and Godly in this present world."* Amen. Hope something was said that can help you may God bless you and keep you.

Your Messenger Jimmy J.

Chapter Forty-Three

GOD is a Jealous *God*

Praise the Lord Saints because He's worthy of all praises due unto him

1 John 1:9 *"If we confess our sins, he is faithful and just to forgive us our sins, and to cleanse us from all unrighteousness."*

God is a Jealous God, and he's the lover of our soul he loves his children very much. He is love, and he don't like it when we take our eyes off him, and start looking for love in all the wrong places because the love we find may not be genuine, some look for love in the club, some find they love in drugs, and some find that they love drinking out of that bottle, many of us love cars and clothes the majority of us are infatuated with the love of money. But I speak as a messenger of God and say to those that have found Jesus have found the most greatest love of all, there is no one who can love better and take care of you, protect you, and give you the desires of your hearts. God looks past our faults, shortcoming and see our needs. God is a good god he sits high on the throne looks down low and sees all of our wrongs, God is a Just God who full of mercy and grace, I thank God for having mercy on me and picking me up out of the mess I was in giving me another chance time and time again to get it right and live for him Amen.

He already knows that many of us who are trying to live the Christian life do not line up to the measure of his standards of what it means to live right. Many of us are going to come up short, but God loves us unconditionally, in spite of our wrong doings, our profane speaking, our perverse thinking being stubborn and against what's right or sensible. God loves us in spite of the things we do that's not pleasing his eye sight. God do not want us to put nothing or no one before him, God wants us cherish his love and keep our minds on him, and the things above. He wants to be the center of our attention, because all things in heaven and earth revolve around him.

Let us stay focus and keep our eyes on the prize, that prize is Jesus Amen. As long as we look to Jesus and follow after him and his ways, it would be hard for us to get lost and lose his way in life, because he the way and he is life, he's a way maker when it seems like you just can't make it God will see you through and bring you over. Amen.

God will bring you over and see that you make it through the hard times of the lack of money and food, and the things you need. He sent Jesus into the world to be our savior, and He will provide he's bread in a staving land, he the bread of life and abridge over trouble water, he's peace in a mist of a storm he's a doctor to those who are sick and call on him and trust him for a healing, he's a lawyer in the court room who's able to get you out of trouble that you brought on yourselves. Jesus is everything you need and everywhere at the same time,

Jesus got power, we need to stay connected to that source of power when were plug in to that main line we become like a live wire, and if you touch one who is plug in to that main source of power you will feel God power going all through your body. Its power in the love of God his love can change you from walking contrary and living a negative life to living a positive life and doing things that are necessary for Christ, such as being obedient and striving to live right or testify about the goodness of the Lord, helping people in need by giving or sharing what you have when you barely have enough for yourselves God will provide, and he is not to be put on a shelf he is to be displayed so other will see the beauty of the Lord. Abiding in you as you put yourself on display to be used by the master. Amen

That which we have seen and heard we declare unto you ye also may have fellowship with us; and truly our fellowship is with the father and his son Jesus Christ. God loved us first even when we did not have no mind to come to church, he loved us first, even when we were out in the world being rebellious and doing our on thing, he redeemed us and set us free with his precious blood when Jesus died for us on Calvary. So as we live from day to day and try to unravel our lives from being wrapped up in sin, caught up in a world of lust of disobedient people tied to a world of greed. Where the majority of people only look out for themselves and only a few of them looks out to the people who are in need.

But that's the world we live in, God created this world and he created us to live and bring glory unto him we are his children and we belong to him. God is a jealous God and he does not want us to put nothing or no one before him. May you spread love, not hate or greed take heed to his spoken word and put him first in your life let him be your guild trust in God and he will always be there for you to help you, heal you, and deliver you from some of the troubles you face from day to day to day.

He also said if I be for you who can be against you, if you have God on your side nothing or no one shall prevail, he said if I be for you no weapon form against you shall prosper if God got your back and stand before you and at your side he's on top of the whole situation he will protect you and keep you safe while we are worry about a certain situation God has already figured it out. God is a awesome God and he's worthy to be praised. He loved us even when we did not love ourselves, many people of the world do not like or love them selves because of the wrongs they done in their life, but God loves us unconditional and he's a forgiving God. When Jesus died on the cross he died for all of our sins, so no one should hate their selves instead hate the sin in you Amen, and love yourself. Show more love toward God and others love yourself and put God first in your life because God is a jealous God.

May God bless you and keep you hope something was said that may help you through God spoken word in plain view written just for you.

Capernaum_Galilee2

Chapter Forty-Four

It's a shortages in the power system

Praise the Lord Saints, and thank him for regenerating what was once dead, has been brought back to life, through the power of God's word.

Many of us who are connected to the power of God's word have had a failure in staying connected to that main-line of communication, which is Jesus our main source of getting through to the Father God Almighty. There's a defect running along the lines of our minds. Causing a shortages in the power system, that cause it to go off and come back on due to the loose connection, Just the same as us who are striving to stay focus and on course with God's word but we have a tendency of getting off track, and back on Corse again. The majority of us today are trying to operate our minds and function with a loose connection that causes us to act u p and not play right and abide by God's rules. Because there's a defect in the lines of our minds, or because we're not plug all the way in to that main source of power. We still have a shortage in the power system. God Almighty, the Father God in Heaven, is a very mighty and powerful God. Who is the source of our power, we the people of God and the people of the world is the system which God use's to reach his people and deliver his word, so that it may be heard throughout the world, unto every man, women, boy and girl. But it seems to be a shortages spreading GOD'S word across to reach the lost. That's because many of our wires our faulty and defected. And need to be renewed and reconnected to carry God power that runs along the lines of our minds too much power flowing through one line may cause it to blow a fuse, so let us spread God power unto others so they too will be able to use that same power flowing along the lines of our minds. May you find ways to redirect some of that power to others? May you spread the power of God word through a separate line, so others will also benefit from the high boost of power, which turns on the power of joy, and lift your spirit up fill your minds with the juice of God's power. That's the good juice that bares good fruit. The juice in that power also brings light unto all that's house, and you will shine as light in dark places Amen.

The power of God word will bring you out of darkness into the marvelous light.

St John 1-12, *"In the beginning was the word and the word was with God, and the same was in the beginning with God, and the word was with GOD."*

That tells me that the word is Jesus, and Jesus was with God and the word was God, they both are one in the same. And without him was not anything made that was made in him was life, and that life was the light of men.

V.5 *"And that light shined and the darkness comprehended it not."*

This mean that we the children of God walking in the light surrounded with evil, and people walking in darkness all around us doing every imaginable thing under the sun grieving God spirit. We who are walking in the light of God power do not hath to be taking with the evil around us and take part in all the darkness of evil thing going on around us. Amen.

There was a man sent from God whose name was John. The same came to bear witness of the light. He was not that light, but was sent to bear witness of that light. If the power of light has shined in your life, then we too can bear witness of that light that was the true light, which lit up every man that comes into the world.

V.10 *"He was in the world and the world knew him not."*

V.11 reads *"But as many as received him to them he gave power to become sons of God, even unto them that believe on his name."*

Today is the same as it was back in the olden days when men and women walked among Jesus and sat in various places he spoke at, and taught people how to live right. But many did not receive his word. The same as us today in the new modern world is still rejecting his word that been taught in various places today. We the people of today are still rejecting God's word. We have ears to hear with and listen not. Unto what thus said the Lord? And that same disobedient and unbelief is following along the lines of our minds here and now in this world, we live in. Amen.

Chapter Forty-Five

Being about God's Business

John 9:4-5 *"I must work the works of him that sent me, while it is day; the night cometh when no man can work. As long as I am in the world I am the light of the world."*

Praise the Lord Saints, and thank him for his love, mercy and grace.

Glorify your Father in heaven. If you are a child of God the father in heaven, and you're striving to live right, constantly telling people about the goodness of God. Let us not just talk about the goodness of God, but also be about what we talk about. Amen. If were saying God is a good God and he's good all the time I know this because he being good to me, if God love and goodness has being spread to you then you should make it your business to spread his love and goodness to others. If we say God is worthy of all honor and praise due unto him, then let us make it our business to honor one another, and give respect to show love to others. Like God showed his love unto you, may you give encouragement to others to strengthen each other, and also make those who feel unworthy feel worthy. God said in his word what you do to each other the same is done unto me. May we all bring honor and praise to the Father in heaven. Amen

Let us the fellow servants of God make it our business to do good to others as often as we can. If were saying God is able, I know God is able to do all things except fail. Reason I know because he fixed for me when I fail myself. He brought me a mighty long way if we know God brought us a mighty long way let us help bring others to the way of learning to live a righteous life. So they too will be able to say God is a able God the reason I know because when I was down he pick me up, many will say they know God is able because when my mind was mess up and confused he regulated my mind and straight it out.

Others will say I know God is real because when I did not have no food to eat he put food on my table when I was not able to provide for myself. Some will say they know God is able because when they couldn't pay they bills, all they had to do is look to the hills which cometh the help which is Jesus, and he stepped in and sent the help that was needed. He step into a bad situation and made it better. Jesus have help us make it over and brought us a mighty long way. So may we help others make it over and bring them along the way with us? Amen. As we walk along this tedious journey let us be about God business. May we strive to be about God business so that he may count us worthy? So that we may be counted in that number among the righteous. Many of us talk the talk of being righteous and Holy Ghost filled, but yet in still when it comes to walking the walk and lining up with God's word, and measuring up to the kind of person God is calling for us to be, we all fall short in meeting up to his standard, and living according to the way he desires for us to live.

That's why we must stay in the word and continue to learn his ways,so that we ourselves will walk according to his ways and be about God's business so that we may have a closer walk with Jesus. Amen.

If we are going to be apart of God's army we must put on our war clothes and prepare for battle. If your constantly struggling and fighting battle after battle, and your moving at God command, you're a soldier that's in it to win it, letting the world know who grounds your standing on and who you are fighting for. Those standing on holy grounds are standing on good grounds. Everyone standing with Jesus shall be more than a conquer, he said in his word no weapon form against you shall prosper. Let us be about God business, he will fight our battles and bring us the victory over the battles in our life. He also said who can be against if I be for you. Even though the battles of war may arise in your life, you can defeat them all through the strength of Jesus Amen. And you will get the victory over each battle in your life keep the faith and continue to fight. 1John 5:4-8 say **"For whatsoever is born of God overcomes the world even our faith. Who is he that overcomes the world, but he that believe Jesus is the son of God. This is he that came by water and blood, even Jesus Christ; not by water only, but by water and blood, and it is the spirit that bears witness, because the spirit is truth. There are three who bear record in heaven, the father, the word and the Holy Ghost; these trees are one. And there are three that bear witness in earth, the spirit the water, the blood, and these three agree in one."**

May we who are on earth come to agreement with God's word, and share his word with one another, study his word and strive to live his word so that we may be about our father business who sits high on throne looking down on us to carry on and follow the footstep of Jesus known as the son of man king of kings and Lord of Lords.

Jesus himself said to his mother how is it that you look for me ye not know that I must be about my Father business. That was after his parents had left him behind they went back to look for him, and found sitting in a temple being about his father business, in the mist of doctors talking and asking question.

One day Jesus is going to come back looking for us asking questions, may we be found walking worthy being about God business following after righteousness so when he sound the trumpet and call the roll call of all the names of the righteous and unrighteous will your name be among the righteous to come go with Jesus or will you be left behind, because you were not about your father business

2 Timothy 1:9 reads *"Who hath saved us and call us with an holy calling not, according to our works but according to his own purpose and grace, which was giving us in Christ Jesus before the world began, but now is made manifest by the appearing of our savior Jesus Christ."*

Who abolished death, meaning he put a end to death, and hath brought life and immortality to light through the gospel many of us lived in immorality meaning to have a bad mind or spirit and conduct ourselves wrongfully with the wrong mind and spirit because we were blind spiritually and could not see but through the gospel. God gave light to help us see how to live a better way and conduct ourselves with the right mind and spirit to be about God business.

Isaiah 1:18-19 *"Come now and let us reason together, saith the Lord; though your sins be as scarlet they shall be as white as snow; though they be red they crimson they should be as wool. If ye be willing and obedient, ye shall eat the good of the land; but if ye refuse and rebel ye shall be devoured, with the sword for the mouth of the Lord has spoken it."*

To be devoured is to be consumed, meaning we will be destroyed, back then people where devoured with the sword, but in today's world many different weapon and devices to be devoured by if we fail to be obedient to God word refuse the precious gift of life wrap in love giving to you from our father above. John 3:16 say *"That God so loved the world that he gave his only begotten son, that whosoever believed in him shall not perish, but have everlasting life."* Amen.

If you believe God sent his son from Heaven to earth to save the lost and die among the people for the sins of the world, if anyone believes this to be true then that someone should be glad to know we have a savior.

Somebody should glad in they heart about what Jesus did for us; I know I'm glad about it. It's good to know we have somebody who will protect you and keep you safe from hurts, harmful dangerous, situations. If were really glad about what Jesus done for us let us be about our father God business, meaning we are going hath to go the work for the Lord, to be about his business let us show up on time to meet God on the daily basic and study his word. 2 Timothy 2:15 say *"Study to show*

thyself approve unto God a workman that need not be a shamed rightly dividing the word of truth." Praise the Lord the word gives us knowledge and helps us in all aspects of life. May we be knowledgeable enough to know we cannot live on bread alone? We must also be fed the word of God to be about God business, we must also be mindful of others. Being about God's business means we must help one another.

Love is the doorway through which the human soul passes from selfish to servant, from solitude to sharing God's love with a multitude.

Testimonial page

My name is Jimmy Jordan I live in St. Louis Mo.

I've been diagnose with diabetes, prostate cancer, and I have been shot in the back of the head, On Feb, 26. 1989 3:oo a:m the bullet came through the back window of the truck I was driving. It hit me in the lower back part of my head I fell over the steering wheel of the truck, my feet smash on the gas pedal, not knowing where I was going, unable to drive. I crashed the truck, the police got me out of the truck laid me on the ground face down. Blood was running out of the wound in my head. I stuck my finger back over the hole, trying to stop the bleeding, but of course it kept on bleeding. My eye's felt heavy, all I could do was call on Jesus and ask Him to keep my eyes opened. I called him over and over Jesus don't let my eyes close because I knew if they would have closed that night at that hour, I would have never seen day light again. God kept my eyes open until the ambulance arrived. They put me on the stretcher into the ambulance. Jesus road with me to the hospital until I was in the care of a doctor. God saved my life, the doctor said I had A 50/50 chance of living. God gave me favor and decided to let me live. I am also the survivor of two different brain surgeries, God also regulated my blood sugar level, and healed me from cancer, brought me through 36 treatments of radiation, delivered me from drug use, tobacco, and from drinking beer every day.

Thank you Jesus, I am now 13 years clean, sober and living for God.

Hi my name is Ethel Jordan; I'm the mother of the messenger Jimmy Jordan

God is a healer; I am a member of the Crusade for Christ Christian Church Home. Pastor Earl Jordan is the Pastor, I was diagnosed with Breast Cancer in 2001, I had cancer in both breast. The doctor said that I had too many lumps in both breast for them to reach in and take the lumps out, so the only thing they could do was to remove both breasts, but I refused to let them do that. So they did not. I continued my visits to the Doctor, because I prayed for God to heal me, and I believed he would. I carried the cancer for 4yrs, without seeing a doctor. The Lord grew what looked like to me a large blister on the outside of my breast. I never told anyone. About a month before the Lord brought it to a head, pain began to shoot through the breast, I still did not tell anybody, and neither did I go to any doctor. I just continued to pray, and believe that God was going to heal me. I had no doubt, I had no fear. So I kept going until one morning the blister busted, and blood poured. This was after 4yrs, of carrying this, without doctor treating me.

So I went to the hospital and the doctor removed one breast in august, and the other breast was removed in November of that same year. During those 4yrs, of carrying that breast cancer, the lord never let me get sick. I was never in any severe pain. The lord never let me get sick in the 4yrs, before the surgery, and the lord never let me get sick after the surgery. I am now 82 yrs, old and still going. I carried it before the surgery and he never let me get sick after the surgery. If you have a problem or some type of illness, just have faith, and trust in God he will deliver you. May God bless you and keep you forever. Sister Ethel Jordan.

I'm Pastor Earl Jordan. I was born into a Christian family, with a mother and father that believed in God. They took me to church on Sunday we sung songs, prayed and I learned about Jesus Christ. As I became older, I started hanging out with the guys in our neighborhood. We started to get into trouble, years later I became homeless living in the streets or wherever I could. I was in and out of many drug treatment centers that did not work for me; I was killing myself slowly until one day I looked into my mother eyes. God let me see the pain, emotional distress that I caused; I knew that my family loved me and that they were praying for me. Then I begin to pray to God for forgiveness and deliverance came. Since that day I haven't been the same. God change my life and gave me a better insight on life. He called me out of the world into the Kingdom business, gave me leadership and made me Pastor of the Crusade for Christ Christian church home. I thank God for saving me in Jesus name. Amen.

Hi my name is sister, Jean Beal's Brown

This is my testimony, of trials and tribulations.

I was a hopeless case, a drug user; crack cocaine was my choice of drug. I felt as though I had no mind, and felt very hopeless in life. But God had a purpose for my life, but I had to go through some things in order to know God for myself.

In June of 1997 I was born again under the leadership of Pastor Jeff Johnson Jr. After being born again, I still did not know the value of it, so I went back out in the world drugging and drinking, not caring about life itself. I was killing myself, so blind to the truth. In 1998 God called my 25 year old daughter home with him. That still did not stop me from getting high.

As life went on, things got worse for me. I had become ill with cancer in the year of 2000, but God being the God he is delivered me out of the love he has for me.

In 2001 I went back to God and asked for forgiveness, He forgave all of my wrong doing, and I thank him for that. As time went on things got better.

I was free from drugs and cancer, now in 2009, the cancer came back.

It was a very hard battle to fight, I had to undergo chemo& radiation for six weeks, I was sick all the time during the treatment and God allowed me to go back to being an infant. I couldn't do anything for myself; I could not eat, sit up or walk without help. I was on medication for pain because I couldn't cope with the pains, but God is still good. He gave me a husband to take care of me.

My husband did not know how to take care of his self, let along taking care of a sick wife; But God worked through the pastor, gave him everything he needed to get the job done. He had to take me back and forth to the doctor, work a job, come home and feed me, bathe me, walk with me. He gave me my medicine, and the main thing he had to do was pray for me. When I was too sick to pray for myself, our pastor told me to keep the faith. To remember what God had already done! Surely he was He able to take care of me in this situation.

He said don't give up, he also prayed for me and my husband, that God would keep us both. God deliver me off of drugs, and healed my body from cancer, I am truly free today. I thank God for my pastor and my husband today, if it had not been for God working through the pastor telling me to hold on and keep the faith I would not be here, it was faith in God that kept me through my darkest days. God kept me, and in my darkest hour he gave me hope so no matter what you go through God is a keeper. In my darkest days I got to know God for myself so I thank God for dark days and every day. I am free to this day, free of cancer and free from drugs.

Sister Jean Beals Brown.

Testimony of Thomas Bracken

I truly and sincerely give God Almighty the praise and the glory for the opportunity to tell the world about the grace of God, I am a sinner and I have lived the life of a sinner for about 55 years of my life, I have done about everything that you can think of that would classify me as sinner in the eyes of God. I once was a alcoholic, and I used to smoke I had a very nasty talking mouth, every other word that came out of my mouth was a foul word.

I had no respect for anyone: I use to hurt people for no reason just because I could get away with it. I was raised in a Christian home, my mother and grandmother were Christian, they taught me about the Father God Almighty and his son Jesus, when I was growing up; and when I became a young man of the age of 17 years old I became a man who found sin in a big way and loved it, I loved serving the devil at that time in my life. But one day when I was around 55 years old and visiting my female friend.

I started feeling strange, I did not know what was happening to my body, but I felt it would pass, but it did not pass I started to feel worst, I was having a heart attack. My lady friend knew what was happening, because she was a nurse. I passed out and woke up in the hospital; the doctor said that I had died; I remember being somewhere that had nothing to do with the physical side of life. I was in a spirit form, I was wondering where my body was.

I couldn't see it. I was also wondering, where was I? There was darkness all around me, but in the mist of the darkness there was a light. I felt that I must pass through the light to get home. I felt love all around me. I felt no pain, I had no fear, and death had a sweet taste to it. I began to float toward the light and then I heard someone calling my name, *Thomas, Thomas. Thomas.*

I stopped floating toward the light and started floating back to the voice that was calling my name. Then all of a sudden I was back in my body, I opened my eyes and I was in the hospital. The doctor was next to my ear telling me that I had a heart attack. Well after that experience I have not been the same person I used to be. My whole life changed and I gave God almighty and his son Jesus Christ all the praise and Glory. Amen.

Testimony of former pastor of Time Is Now

Hi my name is Mrs. Armiltha Williams, of St. Louis Mo. I was coming home from downtown on the Cass bus. The bus was full, there were people standing up in the middle of the bus. As we turned the corner, the bus turned the corner on two wheels, almost turning over. I was standing up. I called on Jesus I believe it was 3 times saying *Jesus, Jesus, Jesus*. He heard my cry and the bus stayed up just like the mighty hands of God had took control over the bus. A man said to me, I don't have to ask if you are you a Christian because you called on the right name, the name of Jesus. Then he asked me what church I belonged to. The people on the bus stood around me from every side, greeting me, hugging me, and kissing me, asking me the same question. I will never forget that day. Fragment basket Church

Testimony of Mr. Leon Jones.

I was born in St. Louis Mo., in the Pruitt Igo projects. At the age of 21,

I was shot 5 times, 2 times in the leg, once in the back, once in the arm and 1 time in my finger. I was in intensive care close to coma state for 3 weeks.

I saw a hand that appeared as the hand of God. My life flashed before my eyes, and then I began to get completely healed of all gunshot wounds.

Jimmy Jordan - The Messenger

I started going to church for about 4 yrs until I backslid and started back running the streets of St. Louis.

I began selling drugs and using them myself. I continued doing drugs and working for Satan, our adversary. Later I ended up getting shot in the head leaving me close to death. I was a victim of a robbery. But God saved my life, once again. I am now free from drugs and no longer sell drugs or use them. I am healthy and well, living on my own, in my own place doing fine and praising the Lord on a daily basis.

I was also healed from having a stroke; I also acquired a heart murmur from shoot dope, heroin and cocaine, along with using alcohol daily, like I did in the past.

But thanks be to God I am a new man who no longer does these anymore. With God's blessing and his grace, my heart is doing fine. My blood level is low, and each morning I wake up, I acknowledge God for who He is and for what He has done for me in my life! Amen.

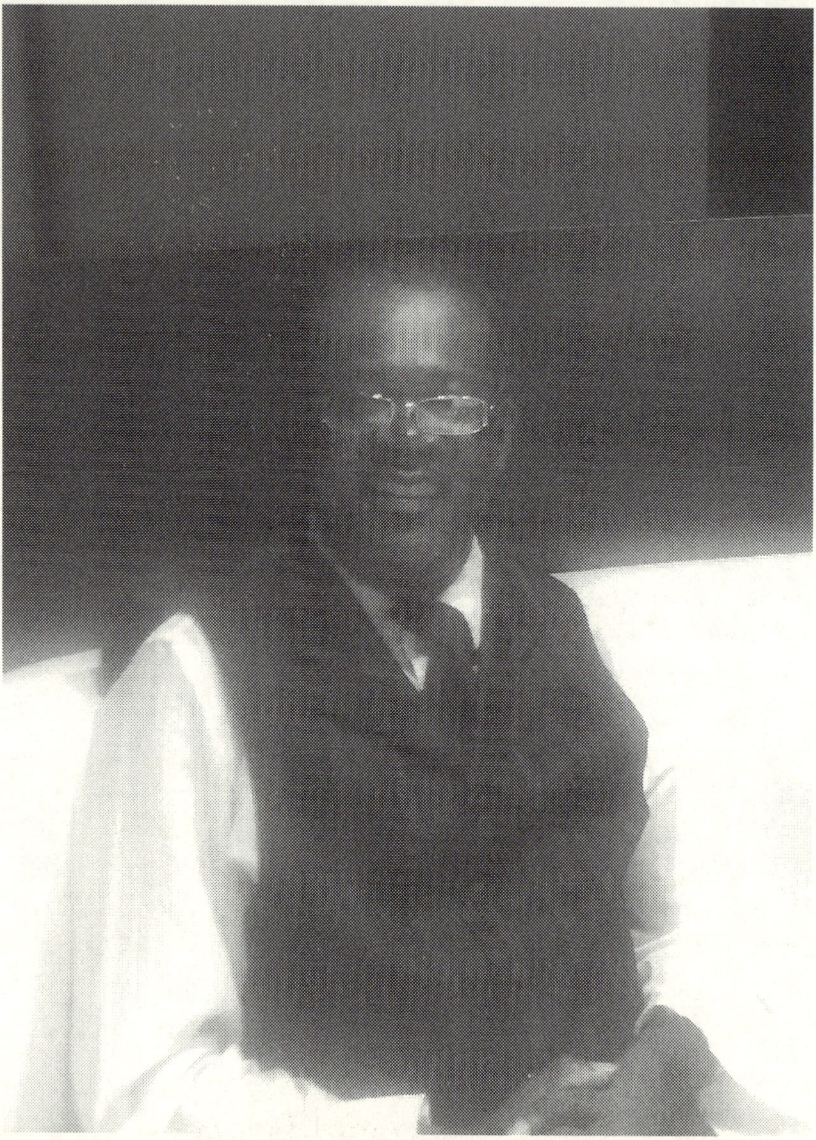

My Biography

My name is Jimmy Jordan; I grew up on the north side of the city of St. Louis MO. I was born in the Pruitt I" go projects. I come from a family of 7, 5, boys and 2, girls I am the youngest of the family, my family showed me much love growing up, I experience hard times at a early age, my mother and father both are Christians. The neighborhood I grew up in was rough, shooting and killings went on continuously, along with stealing and fighting, drinking and drugging, mugging/ robberies and burglaries. But God saw fit to keep the Jordan family safe. I was considered *cool* when I was in school, and to those who knew me. When I was in school I ran with the bad boys doing bad things, but I have always had a good heart, my love for God has always been a big part of my life, even though sometimes I did wrong.

I have always repented and asked God for his forgiveness. I was brought up in church, I was taught many teachings about the Christian life I was also taught by others how to live the worldly life. And experienced the so called fun of running the streets, I had a few girlfriends and many days and nights of fun. My mother and father never had much money, but they managed to provide and take care of all seven of us with the little they had. I have seen my mother go many days without, to give her children what they need. Some say I'm bullheaded because I never seem to listen when someone is trying to tell me something to help me. But now I have a better mind and take time to listen more to what other have to say. My disobedient cause me to get shot in the back of the head, but thanks be to God I was not pronounce dead the God I serve saved me and let me live, not long after that I begin to listen what God was saying to me as well as others who were speaking positive things in my life, I now have the mind to listen and learn.

I shared 15yrs. of my life with a woman by the name of Donna Lynn Coney, who loved me dearly and she is very close to my heart. My love for her remains, but our relationship is not the same as it use to be, but we still have love for one another and we are still close friends. Amen.

I am a writer, I write down the things God speaks into my life, that's how I became The Messenger, by writing down His messages and speaking on them. Most of them were my mess, that I allowed God to use me to turn my mess into a message to encourage others to do better and take heed to God's word. Amen.

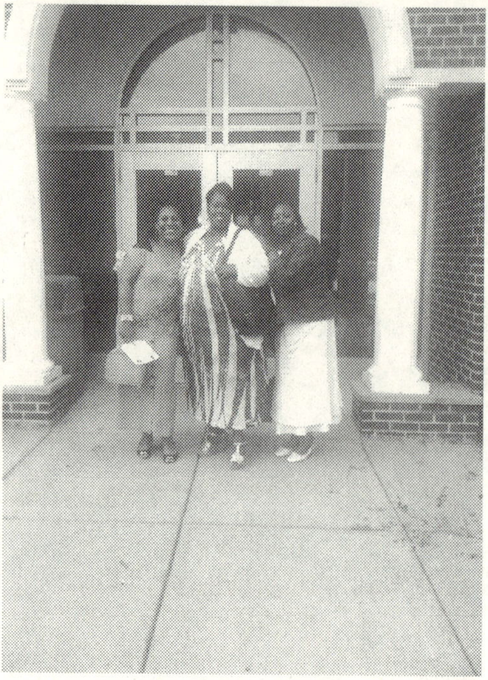

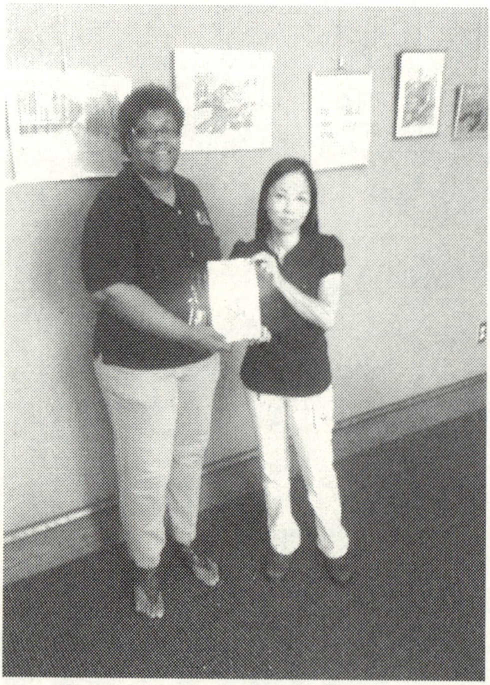

Acknowledgements

First and foremost I the Messenger Jimmy Jordan give thanks to God Almighty, who makes all things possible, dreams and goals reachable for us to hold. I thank him for giving me the mind to write this book God spoken word in plain view, so that more of his word may be heard through reading this book. I thank God for all the many different things he done for me in my life I thank him for my mother and father; I truly thank him for the word of God that was instilled in me at a early age. I also thank him for my brother Pastor Earl Jordan of the Crusade for Christ Christian Church home, who also encourages me down through the years to exercise my gift of speaking by encouraging me to speak God word, which later resulted in me writing God word and encouraging others Amen. I thank my close friend donna/baby just for being a friend and more. I give thanks to Rev. Jeff Johnson Jr., also known as Bro. Jab Pastor of Circle of Light church, where I was also taught tremendous amount of knowledge about the word of God from a man who is greatly filled with the spirit of God and very well verse in scriptures with much knowledge. I give thanks to Renitra Woods who helped me in a big way when I started writing this book, I give thanks to Rochelle my sister in Christ of the Crusade for Christ Christian Ministry Church home, who was willing to help me put this book together, I thank her for her input and all she did in helping me write this book God spoken word in plain view. I give thanks to Sister Chrystal Wagner who is very knowledgeable and skillful in using a computer who was willing to share her expertise with me and let God use her skills to help me write this book. And I give a special thanks to St. Louis Public Library and the staff at the Schlafly and Buder branch, who helped me tremendously with things I did not understand about the computer and malfunctions I encountered doing the production of my manuscript in producing this great book of God's spoken word, written by Jimmy Jordan the Messenger.